59 HOURS

Simon True: Real Stories. Real Teens. Real Consequences.

Simon True

59 HOURS

JOHNNY KOVATCH

SIMON PULSE

NEW YORK LONDON TORONTO SYDNEY NEW DELHI

SIMON PULSE

An imprint of Simon & Schuster Children's Publishing Division

1230 Avenue of the Americas, New York, New York 10020

First Simon Pulse edition March 2018

For information about special discounts for bulk purchases, please contact

Simon & Schuster Special Sales at 1-866-506-1949 or business@simonandschuster.com.

The Simon & Schuster Speakers Bureau can bring authors to your live event. For more information

or to book an event contact the Simon & Schuster Speakers Bureau at 1-866-248-3049 or visit our

website at www.simonspeakers.com.

Cover designed by Sarah Creech

Interior designed by Greg Stadnyk

The text of this book was set in Chaparral Pro.

Manufactured in the United States of America

2 4 6 8 10 9 7 5 3 1

Library of Congress Cataloging-in-Publication Data

Names: Kovatch, Johnny, author.

Title: 59 hours / by Johnny Kovatch.

Other titles: Fifty-nine hours

Description: New York : Simon Pulse, [2018] | Series: Simon true : Real stories. Real teens. Real

consequences. | Audience: Age: 14+ | Includes bibliographical references.

Identifiers: LCCN 2017005186 (print) | LCCN 2017037000 (eBook) | ISBN 9781481476607 (hc) |

ISBN 9781481476591 (pbk) | ISBN 9781481476614 (eBook)

Subjects: LCSH: Hollywood, Jesse James—Juvenile literature. | Markowitz, Nick , 1984-2000—

Juvenile literature. | Murder—California—Santa Barbara—Juvenile literature. | Drug dealers—

California—Los Angeles—Juvenile literature.

Classification: LCC HV6534.S33 (eBook) | LCC HV6534.S33 K68 2018 (print) |

DDC 364.152/3092—dc23

LC record available at https://lccn.loc.gov/2017005186

For the innocent lives lost to senseless violence . . .
and the redemption of those who committed it

CONTENTS

CONTENTS

WHO'S WHO

Victim

Nick Markowitz: fifteen years old

Family

Susan Markowitz: forty years old, Nick's mother

Jeffrey Markowitz: Nick's father

Ben Markowitz: twenty-two years old, Nick's half brother

Jack Hollywood: father of Jesse Hollywood

Defendants

Jesse James Hollywood: twenty years old, marijuana dealer, ordered shooting, sentenced to life without parole, currently housed at Calipatria State Prison

Ryan Hoyt: twenty years old, shooter, sentenced to death, currently housed on death row at San Quentin State Prison

Graham Pressley: seventeen years old, sentenced to California Youth Authority until age 25

Jesse Rugge: twenty years old, served thirteen years, eleven in state prison

William Skidmore: twenty years old, served nine years in state prison

Law Enforcement

Detective Mark Valencia: Santa Barbara County Sheriff's Office, caught fugitive Jesse James Hollywood

Friends/Witnesses

Natasha Adams: friend of Graham Pressley and Jesse Rugge

Brian Affronti: friend of William Skidmore

Eddy Bachman* (pseudonym): drug dealer

Kelly Carpenter: friend of Graham Pressley and Jesse Rugge

Rosalia de la Cruz Gitau: witnessed Nick's abduction

Richard Dispenza: godfather of Jesse James Hollywood

Carey Evans: friend of Nick Markowitz, pallbearer

Richard Hoeflinger: friend of Jesse Rugge

Stephen Hogg: family attorney of Jesse Hollywood and Jack Hollywood

Jerry Hollywood: Jesse James Hollywood's cousin

Gabriel Ibarra: friend of Richard Hoeflinger

Michelle Lasher: girlfriend of Jesse James Hollywood

Pauline Mahoney: witnessed Nick's abduction

Kirk Miyashiro: Nick's dean of students

John Roberts: friend of Jack Hollywood

Chas Saulsbury: friend of Jesse James Hollywood

Casey Sheehan: friend of Jesse James Hollywood

Legal

Hans Almgren: prosecutor, Santa Barbara District Attorney's Office

Joshua Lynn: prosecutor, Santa Barbara District Attorney's Office

Ronald Zonen: prosecutor, Santa Barbara District Attorney's Office

James Blatt: defense attorney for Jesse James Hollywood

Alex Kessel: defense attorney for Jesse James Hollywood

LIZARD'S MOUTH

THE CRIME SCENE WHERE NICHOLAS MARKOWITZ was shot nine times by a TEC-9, then buried in a shallow grave, is known as Lizard's Mouth rock in Goleta, California. In the near distance, a boulder bears his name as part of a carved memorial. Seven odd-shaped stones comprise a border. Branches with leaves have been placed as a tribute at the memorial.

There's a small boulder with a knee-high tagging of a smiley face, which, after a closer look, isn't smiling at all—its mouth is a single black slit, like a warning to all who enter. At its foot, Camel Crush cigarette butts and Lost Coast Brewery bottle caps. Hikers come here to walk among the massive sandstone outcroppings and watch a majestic sunset over the Pacific. A couple of teens are perched within the band shell of a boulder on the opposite side of where Nicholas was murdered.

Seven years ago, a fire cut a swath through this national forest. Afterward, planes flew over, trying to scatter seeds in an attempt to restore the brush. What couldn't be salvaged was at the mercy of the winds. Nick's memorial survived. *His* name and lifespan are carved into the base of sandstone, beaten down by time and elements trying to reclaim their most natural state or erase the memory of what even fire couldn't erase:

Nicholas

Samuel

Markowitz

9-19-84

8-8-2000

His actual death was on the ninth, but back then that detail was still being disputed. He was fifteen years old.

Over time, observers have paid respects in their own ways. Bottles of Manischewitz wine, soda, makeshift crosses, angel figurines, seashell necklaces. Unforgiving years have scoured raw the orange X investigators spray-painted on a different side of this rock to first mark this site. Now, spray-painted in black:

RIP

NSM

8-8-2000

This boulder recedes into the thicket below Lizard's Mouth rock, a formation resembling a reptile's opened jaw, in the Santa Ynez Mountains. The amphitheater-shaped rock is forty feet high. Climbers choose this location for bouldering opportunities. Over the years, water and wind have carved an intricate maze of caves. Boulders are artistically named—one in particular is called Lord of the Flies, after the novel in which boys on a desert island turned savage and sacrificed one of their own.

Nearby, graffiti has been sprayed onto a ridge. The artwork resembles an eerie creature that's part fish with the antlers of a twelve-point buck. Next to it: *What Have You Seen Today?*

But Nicholas wasn't up there to take in the full moon or commemorate the panorama after a long day of climbing. He wasn't even there by choice. No, he was driven there just after midnight on a summer night in August 2000. His three assailants drove Highway 154 into the Los Padres National Forest to West Camino Cielo and weaved up the road until reaching an altitude of three thousand feet. From there, his six-foot frame and size-fourteen feet were marched to this burial site, a long way from the corner of his abduction at Platt Avenue and Ingomar Street in West Hills, California, just fifty-nine hours before.

Chapter 1

INSURMOUNTABLE

AUGUST 9 HAS BEEN A MEMORABLE DATE THROUGH-
out history.

In 1936 American track star Jesse Owens would add to his
hundred-meter, two-hundred-meter, and long-jump gold medal
performances by capturing his fourth gold medal as part of the
United States 4 x 100 meter relay team at the Summer Olympic
Games in Berlin, where a failed-painter-turned-Führer named
Adolf Hitler was in attendance.

In 1945 American forces would drop a second atomic bomb
on Nagasaki in Japan.

In 1969 five individuals, including actress Sharon Tate, who
was eight and a half months pregnant, would be found murdered
in the wealthy suburb of Benedict Canyon in Los Angeles. Cult
leader Charles Manson, who was not present during the slaughter,
and several of his followers were later convicted of the killings.

And on August 9, 2000? While South African president Thabo Mbeki unveiled a Women's Monument commemorating the role of women in the antiapartheid struggle, Ryan Hoyt, at the command of Jesse James Hollywood, would shoot fifteen-year-old Nicholas Markowitz with a gun converted from semi to fully automatic. The official report: Nicholas was kidnapped a little after one p.m. on August 6, 2000. He was murdered sometime after midnight on August 9 of the same year.

There would be an August 10. Yet it would not be until August 14 that several men in dark suits arrived at the home of Susan and Jeff Markowitz to inform them that they had found their son's body. "It was bullet riddled."

Just like history, there was not a single event that led to this one, but an accumulation, no—an accretion of willful negligence, parental misguidance, CYA or cover-your-ass perspective, and drug-hazed choices that crystallized the chaos. And because of that, August 9 became another memorable day in history for all the wrong and preventable reasons.

Chapter 2

THE ABDUCTED

IN 1987 WESTERN CANOGA PARK OFFICIALLY BECAME West Hills. West Hills was flanked on the north by the Chatsworth Reservoir, on the east by Canoga Park, on the south by Woodland Hills, and on the west by Bell Canyon in Ventura County. In more general terms, it was a little over an hour's drive north to Santa Barbara or a thirty-minute drive south to Malibu. Nicholas knew West Hills well. He was about to know Santa Barbara a whole lot better.

It was one p.m. on a sidewalk near Taxco Trails Park, where Nicholas Markowitz was walking. Nicholas was still growing into his six-foot frame. He was laid-back, charismatic, and personable.

Because of a concrete retaining wall, he couldn't be seen by the residents whose homes bordered the street.

Nicholas had left his house at some point between nine and

eleven a.m. He had snuck out, wanting to avoid a confrontation with his concerned parents. No one knew where he had gone.

Nicholas couldn't turn for advice to his half brother, Ben Markowitz, who was seven years older. Ben had left for Arizona sometime within the previous two days to work a short contracting job for an uncle. Ben would be back in West Hills the following day, Monday, August 7.

Ben, who was often in trouble with the law, was a menacing figure, covered in tattoos. He had a short temper to match. Ben had previously sold marijuana for a local dealer whose birth certificate read Jesse James Hollywood. Yes, this was his real name. Jesse's father, who was twenty-four years old at the time, named his son after an uncle and admitted it wasn't just happenstance that he would share the name of the famous nineteenth-century outlaw.

Ben Markowitz's feud with Hollywood over Ben's drug debt had reached its peak. Before he left for Arizona, Ben had smashed the windows of Hollywood's home.

In one part of town, Nicholas's older brother had provoked a conflict two days before on August 4, while two days later on August 6, Nicholas was walking away from his parents' home to avoid one. Both would culminate at the intersection of Ingomar and Platt, at one p.m. on that lethargic Sunday afternoon when a dented, white-paneled, windowless '91 Chevy van suddenly swerved curbside.

Three young men who had been friends from childhood were in it. Jesse Rugge was the driver. Rugge was six foot four, with an athlete's lean build and effortless charisma. Hollywood was in the passenger seat and William Skidmore in the back. Skidmore was viewed as the "body man" of the group. With impressive musculature and quick hands, Skidmore never shied away from a fight or from backing up his friends during one.

The three friends' original destination had been Ben Markowitz's parents' house. They figured Ben had to be there. If they were lucky, maybe they'd see his car out front. They had been calling people, trying to find out where he was. By this time, they had already been drinking a little and had smoked weed. They were buzzed, feeling good.

Skidmore knew Taxco Trails Park—it was where he'd sometimes had batting practice as a little kid. What he wasn't familiar with? Why Hollywood was ordering the van to pull over. That was when Jesse spotted Ben's brother. Nicholas was headed back in the direction of his home less than a mile away. William was surprised. He didn't even know Ben had a brother.

Jesse James Hollywood emerged from the passenger seat and opened the back door. Nicholas was at first relieved to see Hollywood's face. "What's up, Jesse?" he called out to Hollywood. Hollywood pinned Nicholas up against a pear tree in the middle of the sidewalk. Hollywood was looking for Ben because of the drug debt and because he was tired of feeling harassed. Instead he would end up finding Nicholas. Alone. Pager in pocket. Father's ring on his finger.

Hollywood punched Nicholas and screamed at him, asking where he could find his older brother. He then announced, "Grab him!" Skidmore followed his command. He corralled the teen by the collar and forced him into the van, where an AR-15 assault rifle was concealed under a blanket. Nicholas never made an attempt to flee. It would have been futile even if he had tried— you could only open the back sliding door from the outside.

Nicholas hadn't committed some unforgivable act that left twenty-year-old shot-caller Hollywood no choice. He wasn't moving in on Hollywood's territory. He hadn't previously robbed Hollywood during a drug deal gone wrong. No, this teen who would sing Queen's "Bohemian Rhapsody" in the shower, who could memorize fifty pages of Shakespeare in one sitting for drama club, then grease door handles at home as a prank, was held as collateral for his older brother's drug debt.

Once inside, all eyes turned to Hollywood, including Rugge, who was driving. They all wanted to know—*What was the plan?* But even Hollywood hadn't thought that far ahead.

Chapter 3

ORIGIN: JESSE JAMES HOLLYWOOD

TEAM PHOTOS SHOW FOUR FRIENDS—ALL BETWEEN seven and eight years old—who played on the same Little League team called the Pirates. Ryan Hoyt was the first baseman; Jesse Rugge, a clutch infielder; William Skidmore covered the outfield; and Jesse James Hollywood would command the mound as pitcher. Hollywood's father, Jack, coached the team. Their next major picture would not be one posing with their team, but instead, separate booking photos for the Santa Barbara Police Department.

At fourteen, Hollywood sometimes wore his ball cap tilted gang-like to the side during varsity games.

Now these former teammates were years removed from double plays and stealing bases, addicted to prestige and power, which were exactly what Jesse James Hollywood possessed. Though he was only five-four, he compensated for his small stature with a healthy ego and cocky smirk.

Not even out of his teens, he owned a two-hundred-thousand-dollar house, dated a girl who willingly tattooed his name across the small of her back, and owned firearms he'd purchased from cocaine dealers.

Hollywood also had a tricked-out silver '95 Honda Accord DX coupe. It was quoted at thirty-five thousand dollars, thanks to customized hydraulics, neon lights inside the trunk, and mirrored glass.

But when Hollywood wanted to drink, he would rent a limousine to ferry him to collect that night's drug debt. It wasn't as if he needed to be in class that next day. He had been kicked out for fighting or suspended from his share of high schools. That only gave Hollywood more time to move ten thousand dollars a month in vacuum-sealed British Columbian marijuana, so *dank* you could smell it through two Ziplocs.

In a home video shot earlier in 2000, Hollywood wore a Los Angeles Dodgers baseball cap backward. His head was tilted, probably from ingesting Herculean amounts of weed and Heinekens, but maybe also from an arrogance arising out of a sense of entitlement. Though this party took place in his own neighborhood, he fronted as if he was from another, speaking street jargon:

"Down the street, cuz," he began, stating that someone "hit me up, cuz." He followed with, "I'm like, 'What up, cuz?'" He went on to say that this person then "straight ran my ass over, bounced on hydraulics twenty-seven times. That's why I'm a little fucked up right now." He touched the side of his cap with the knuckle of a bent index finger.

"Hydraulics" referred to the customized suspension that can make a car hop an easy six feet in the air, courtesy of seventy-two-volt pumps. And in this case, it was being used as a weapon in his heroic survival narrative. "Still alive, cuz." And the use of "cuz"? A Crips hit-up. Though he lived within the boundaries of Bell Canyon, Canoga Park, and Chatsworth Reservoir, did Hollywood interact with any Crips neighborhoods like the more notorious ones that were twenty-six miles south of West Hills?

When partying, girls, and drinking became too debilitating, the group would pop Viagra to thwart "whiskey dick." When they weren't partying, they would watch heist movies like *Heat*, enamored of its criminal efficiency. All Hollywood needed to live out that fantasy of becoming a criminal mastermind was a loyal crew to run his enterprise. Some thought Hollywood was inspired down this path by his father, who the Santa Barbara County Sheriff's Office believed was running his own marijuana drug ring. A rule of thumb in drug dealing is to pick a crew you trust. What better individuals than the very ones you grew up playing Little League with?

If only seven-year-old Jesse James Hollywood had known while he fingered the seams for his next fastball that he was thirteen years away from becoming the youngest person ever to appear on the FBI's Most Wanted list, a seventy-thousand-dollar price tag placed on his capture.

Chapter 4

THE FEUD

THE ORIGIN OF HOLLYWOOD AND BEN'S FEUD TOOK place in San Diego around February 2000. A friend of Ben's owed Hollywood money. Ben went with Hollywood to collect. Hollywood wasn't going to do his own dirty work. Plus, Ben looked the part of someone not to be messed with. He had a shaved head and intimidating tattoos.

They drove Hollywood's black Mercedes-Benz and brought along a baseball bat and a roll of duct tape.

When they arrived in San Diego, Ben set up a scheme with the friend who owed Hollywood. His friend would bring a dealer who specialized in selling Ecstasy. They would stage a robbery. Ben would "rob" the dealer and tell his friend "to say you got jacked." Ben told his friend that it was better to owe your other friend money than Hollywood. Maybe he was alluding to the fact that owing money to Hollywood came with much more dire consequences. No argument there.

His friend had owed Hollywood two thousand dollars. In lieu of cash, Ben had those two hundred pills from the staged robbery. To incentivize the opportunity, Ben told Hollywood he'd move them, essentially taking on the friend's debt. Ben figured he would come out with four thousand dollars, making two grand for himself after Hollywood's cut, which would have totaled the original debt that he was owed. But Ben only sold six hundred dollars' worth at a party. An hour later, people were coming up to him complaining the E wasn't working. He went back to Jesse's house and gave him the six hundred dollars. He added an extra two hundred dollars from what he made working at his father's company as a machinist.

Ben asked Hollywood what he wanted to do now. Hollywood wasn't happy. He put the remaining twelve-hundred-dollar debt on Ben.

Ben couldn't believe Hollywood would get angry over it. After all, the two had grown close during the previous year, lifting weights together daily. Ben had even lived with Hollywood beginning sometime in November 1999 and ending sometime in February 2000. And now? Ben didn't think Hollywood was this heartless. He didn't understand what was happening.

What was happening was that this twelve-hundred-dollar debt would fester over the next six months. It was less about the money, and more about the point that Ben never attempted to pay Hollywood back. Hollywood felt that Ben had been purposely avoiding him.

Ben believed Hollywood was also hurt by the fact that he stopped selling and hanging with him. He was done with the days of dealing under Hollywood, which included being fronted weed on consignment. Ben had realigned his focus. He was now working every day from six a.m. until two thirty p.m. for his father.

That didn't mean Hollywood was done with him. In April 2000—some two months after Ben and Hollywood's relationship officially soured—Hollywood walked into BJ's Restaurant and Brewhouse on Canoga near Victory Boulevard in the San Fernando Valley. Ben's fiancée, Eliza, who was a server, ended up waiting on Hollywood. Hollywood saw his window to project his frustration. He decided not to the pay the check, instead leaving Ben's fiancée a note reading "Just take this off Ben's debt." Ben's fiancée had to cover the fifty-dollar tab.

After seeing her ring, Hollywood figured out they were engaged. He couldn't believe Ben had money to buy *her* a ring but not pay *him* back. He told Eliza that Ben had been "ducking me."

This set Ben off. The two would go back and forth with phone threats. Ben called Hollywood after the restaurant incident. He called him a little punk and said that Hollywood wasn't getting a dime out of him. In turn, Hollywood would have William Skidmore leave voice mails at two thirty in the morning.

The taunting escalated beyond words. Ben remembered that Hollywood owned a thirty-five-thousand-dollar Honda. He had payback in mind and reported Hollywood for committing insurance fraud after the car was chopped and sold for parts. Ben had been with Hollywood when he purchased the insurance, so he knew the insurance company.

Ben had had enough when he was driving home one night and saw Hollywood and Ryan Hoyt waiting out front of his apartment. He kept on driving with no idea how Hollywood had learned his address. Ben delivered one last voice mail to Hollywood. "I know where you live, too, buddy, so you make the first move." Ben wasn't afraid of Hollywood's inner circle. "They're just a bunch of punks that can't fight worth a lick."

Hollywood's alleged fear gave way to anger after Ben broke his front windows. Skidmore was asleep in the back guest room. They heard a crash and ran out the front door as a car took off. The neighbor across the street said, "Hey, did you guys see that? I think it was a white BMW." They knew it could only be one person.

Skidmore immediately called Ben. He told Ben that Hollywood wanted him to fight Ben. Ben declined, then told Skidmore his problem was with Hollywood, that he didn't have a problem with Skidmore. Skidmore—in his loyalty to Hollywood—fired back, "You do now."

Skidmore handed the phone to Hollywood. Ben had already hung up. Two twenty-year-olds amped on adrenaline and ego would now exchange more than just insults.

This couldn't be worked out amicably. Hollywood had a reputation to maintain. He couldn't be disrespected. What would other dealers or his clientele think if he didn't strike back? Hollywood had to make an example out of anyone who tried to undermine him. He also couldn't leave a blemish on the Hollywood name.

Hollywood had borrowed the white van from John Roberts, a family friend, who had old Mafia ties from his Chicago days. Hollywood had already been in the process of using it to move out of his place while he looked for something new and private. He didn't like people knowing where he lived anymore.

After his windows were broken, Hollywood was fed up with Ben Markowitz, and forty-eight hours later, as his anger simmered, the decision was made. "Let's go find him," was Hollywood's order.

Chapter 5

A BROTHER'S INFLUENCE

NICK WASN'T JUST A SAVANT WHEN IT CAME TO remembering his lines for Shakespeare. He also was astute at picking up on Ben's brooding, rebellious, and sometimes volatile demeanor—no matter how nuanced. This rebellion found its way into Nick, transmitted not only during times they spent together, but heightened even more by his older brother's absence. Ben had already done time in juvenile hall, probation camp, and county jail for crimes ranging from assault with a deadly weapon to grand theft auto. On one occasion, when he was sixteen years old, he split open a man's head with brass knuckles.

Ben's influence would induce both praise and resentment from Nick. And at fifteen, this was a potentially dangerous cross-roads. To his father, Ben was "a cat with nine lives."

Nick yearned to emulate his brother. He wanted to pull off Ben's "urban legend" status. It filtered into him. There was no stopping it. Nick would even grow annoyed if anyone referred to them as half brothers.

Ben Markowitz had chosen a nickname, Bugsy, after the 1930s front-page mobster Bugsy Siegel. He had a seething that couldn't be contained—an unwound coil of ink and anger, no pause button to press. He was Jewish but flaunted white supremacist tattoos.

Ben would disappear for periods of time, sometimes up to six months, after confrontations with his father. After one confrontation, he arrived home covered in tattoos from his shoulder blades down to his ankles. These were visual scars to rebel against the suffering he felt from his parents' divorce.

Benjamin split his time between his parents' homes. His step-mother, Susan Markowitz, would take Ben in whenever there was friction with his biological mother. Susan believed that Ben didn't always feel loved.

By eleven, he was slashing tires and crashing a family friend's car he had decided to take out for a joyride. He was placed on Ritalin and later enrolled in tae kwon do—anything to tame the anger and redirect that seething. He was "jumped in" to a local gang before he hit puberty. This meant he was intentionally allowing himself to be beaten up by current gang members as initiation into the gang. The beating could sometimes last up to sixty seconds or whatever that particular gang decided.

By twelve, he had stolen a car. By thirteen, Susan witnessed him being handed a gun by a friend.

It wasn't just the skinhead and wifebeater motif. Benjamin

had a demeanor that jumped from zero to *fury*, just begging for some unsuspecting soul to look at him wrong.

At times he would resent Nicholas, seven years younger. Nicholas represented what Ben had never had—a stable family.

Ben wouldn't bow to anyone—including Hollywood. However, it was his misplaced anger that would jump-start new trauma. At twenty-two years old, he was burning bridges like Bugsy Siegel. However, unlike the charismatic mobster, the contract wouldn't be on his life, but his innocent brother's.

Nick was now caught up in something in which he had no control. Up to this point, the most worrisome thing on his mind had been the conversation he was dreading with his parents about last night.

"Last night" meant "Saturday night," when Nicholas went out with some friends to CityWalk. CityWalk was a part of Universal Studios theme park, filled with restaurants, bars, movie theaters, and electric billboards that rivaled the Vegas Strip. When the rides closed, the nightlife for teens began.

Nick's curfew was midnight, but he came home at eleven thirty, which surprised his father, Jeff, who wasn't used to Nick coming home early. As Nick walked in the door, Jeff and Susan were right there. As soon as they saw him, they knew there was something wrong—they could see it in his face. His eyes were droopy, and he was *chawing* with his mouth. Jeff asked, "What's going on? Why are you home so early?" Nick responded, "Oh, it didn't go so well."

Susan Markowitz knew her son's behavior. He was high on some type of drug. For Susan, it was a delicate balancing job. How much freedom versus how much discipline? In the past, when she had suspicions about Nick's behavior, she would go through his pockets and drawers, occasionally reading his letters.

That night Nick was wearing a pair of baggy pants with a large pocket in the back. Jeff Markowitz noticed something bulging in the pocket and asked his son what he was carrying. Nick covered up the bulge and told his father it was nothing.

Jeff and Susan confronted him because they wanted to know what was going on. As they approached, Nick ran out of the house. It wasn't out of the ordinary for Nick to leave. He'd usually show later in the evening. Other times he would head to his brother's place for a breather, as Ben diagnosed it. In the past, Ben would play mediator between Nick and his parents, then drive Nick home the next day. Jeff and Susan figured he was just going to his brother's for another overnight trip. Unbeknownst to Jeff and Susan, Ben had already left for Arizona to work for his uncle.

Forty-five minutes later, Nick walked back inside. Susan met him with a hug and a kiss. Nick lied, saying that he hated when his parents wanted to talk to him about his smoking. But they knew it wasn't a pack of cigarettes in his pocket. Nick was trying to soften the consequences or save himself from a late-night lecture.

Susan made him a bowl of cereal—one of his favorite late-night snacks—and decided their talk could wait until the morning.

In the morning, Jeff headed out to his usual Sunday tennis match. When he returned, Susan was busy preparing breakfast. "I guess we have a job ahead of us," Jeff mentioned before asking if she would wake Nick. But when she went to his room, he wasn't there. Susan thought, *How could he just leave us again without telling us?*

Jeff also had wanted to get to the bottom of things that morning. "That's when it started. That's when the hell started."

When Jeff mentioned getting to the bottom of things, it wasn't just about what had occurred the previous night, August 5. No, something had been growing within Nick for some time.

Jeff Markowitz had hoped that Nicholas—who, after his thirteenth birthday, wanted to be called *Nick*—could see the damage Ben was causing to himself and to others. It was futile. Jeff thought that all Nick could see was "some slight amount of glory. You fall for the tough guy, he's Captain Hero."

Nick had also been arrested during the school year for possession of marijuana. Although it was only residue found in a small Ziploc, it culminated in his getting arrested, fingerprinted, and suspended. Nick tried to talk his way out of being held responsible, saying he was just holding it for a friend. Susan didn't buy his reason. "That's like a girl saying, 'These aren't my birth control pills. I'm just holding them for a girlfriend.'"

Previously, Ritalin had also been in Nick's possession. Ben had had a prescription since he was twelve. Nick had it for recreation. At their 1999 New Year's Eve party, the whole family knew

Nick was on something. Ben confronted him, trying to protect him from the lifestyle he was leading. By that time, the damage was done. Nick "already had a taste for it."

Nick would tell Ben he'd been into fights. But Ben knew he was just trying to be cool in front of his older brother.

Nick did grow up faster because of what Ben was going through. In a journal Nick shared with Susan, he wrote, *I hope Ben changes from what he used to do because sometimes he hung out with the wrong crowd.* This was before Nick started romanticizing Ben's life—or experimenting with it. Gateway *actions*, instead of drugs. "It made Nick more aware of things he probably would not have thought about if it wasn't in his space or household," Susan recalled. She also believed Nick thought she was being too hard on Ben.

Susan wanted to protect Nick from Ben's negative influence. Every time she tried, "he got more defensive."

Nick would perform poorly in school, then receive a letter from his absent brother encouraging his effort to do better. Ben didn't hang out with Nick, but not because he didn't want to. He wasn't *allowed* to, a consequence of being incarcerated at Camp Miller—a probation camp—at the time.

According to Susan, Ben would write how "he's going to come back and be the 'great brother' he's supposed to be" and to "'listen to Mom and Dad because they're right.'"

Susan believed "it was such a conflict . . . and sad that when one kid ends up getting in trouble, the whole family is trying to cope. And when you're young, it's harder because you're having to go to school. . . . At that age, you think, 'Oh, he's a tough guy [Ben], I can be a tough guy, too. Maybe that's cool.'" Could this have simply been Nick dramatizing the unwanted attention? After all, he was an actor. "He was somebody you could put in front of an audience of people and he would be able to make everyone laugh."

Nick could have been misinterpreting a loving and concerned mother as a strict disciplinarian. "There were no problems at home except for trying to protect Nick from Ben. And Nick thought that was a problem."

Susan had no idea that Ben had given Nick thirty Valium pills on the Friday before Nick's kidnapping. That was the same Friday Ben would unleash whatever was brewing underneath and bust out Hollywood's windows.

Two days later, on August 6, Nick avoided that conversation with his parents about the pills and possibly fingering Ben as his supplier. He would also leave home for the very last time. And walk right into the hands of Jesse James Hollywood.

Chapter 6

911

PAULINE MAHONEY WAS DRIVING HER CADILLAC
with her two children, ages six and nine, along with a friend of
theirs, also nine. She was coming from church and approaching the stop sign where she normally made a right to go to her
house, a block away. As she was approaching the stop sign,
she saw a scuffle occurring on the sidewalk across the street.
As she drove closer, she saw that "these boys were beating up
another boy." Hollywood had Nick pinned against the tree.
Skidmore was called out for backup. Pauline thought the beating went on for thirty seconds. There was no way for Nick to
protect himself.

Pauline was between fifty and a hundred feet away. She
slowly approached at five miles per hour. She watched as they
threw Nick into the van. The van took off but had left Hollywood
behind. They stopped for Hollywood to jump back inside.

She squared her rearview to see if the van was going to follow her. For a second, it seemed like it would. Then, as she made a right turn, the van with Nick continued on.

She didn't have a cell phone on her, so she couldn't immediately call 911. Instead she enlisted her boys to help her remember the license number. She was saying the license plate out loud and "kept repeating it over and over."

It was a little before one p.m. Finally, at home, she called 911.

Pauline wasn't the only witness to Nick's abduction.

Her call was followed by one from Rosalia de la Cruz Gitau, a UCLA grad student. She saw the beating but thought the boy was being "jumped in" to a gang. Just like Ben Markowitz had been jumped in, Rosalia thought this teen was intentionally allowing himself to be beaten up as initiation. But this wasn't sixty seconds to earn the street's respect of a lifetime.

The irony? As much as being jumped in propagandized a false sense of respect, Nick would have been luckier if that were the case. No, this wasn't a gang initiation. It was a repercussion. *Collateral damage.* Skidmore horse-collared him by the shirt and picked him up.

However, no law enforcement would come for Nick. *Two* different emergency dispatchers coded the incident incorrectly.

The first dispatcher coded the first call as an assault, not a kidnapping in progress. For whatever reason, the arriving officers on the scene were apparently slow in their response time. They patrolled around Taxco Trails but never pursued it any further once their search came up empty, even though

Pauline told the dispatcher the van was "heading east on Ingomar." They failed to even take Pauline Mahoney's written statement.

An officer did follow up on the van's owner, John Roberts, but misread his address. Was it too much of an inconvenience to call in the address again?

And the second dispatcher? Sent the call out just once as a *for information only* radio broadcast. But the first officer was on the phone with Pauline Mahoney, so he never heard it.

There was no follow-up with the second witness either, as the second dispatcher didn't connect the two calls with each other.

Susan had bought Nick a pager as an early birthday present. With a pager, someone could call and leave a voice mail, but the recipient would have to use a pay phone, landline, or cell to call the pager to hear it. You could also page a number for the recipient to call you back at. (Skidmore and his friends sometimes just messaged using numbers as code words.) There were no smartphones.

This gift to her son came with one ultimatum. Nick always had to return her pages within ten minutes. If he didn't, she would take the pager away—one week for every minute he was late. She tested him twice, even paging him while he was in the house.

Now she was paging him on that Sunday morning. She waited. One minute turned into eleven. Susan didn't know that Nick was no longer in possession of his pager. Pagers didn't come with a built-in GPS locator that pinged off cell phone towers.

Could Nick hear his mother's warning while his pager went off? *I'm taking it away for a week for every minute that you're late calling me back.*

Back in the van, Nick was scared at first. At some point previously, he had briefly met Jesse Hollywood. Nick tried to act laid back, almost relieved. That didn't stop Hollywood from barking out how Ben owed him money. "Where's your brother? I'm trying to find him."

Nick answered Hollywood that he didn't know Ben's location. He did insist, "My brother will pay you, don't worry about it."

As they were driving, Skidmore could see Nick's confidence wane. Skidmore knew Ben wasn't going to pay anyone anything. He also knew Ben owed more than twelve hundred dollars. Skidmore put the figure closer to twenty-four thousand. Other rumors had it at thirty-six thousand.

Hollywood would press Nick again, and Nick would grow hesitant and nervous. And then, with zero belief, he'd say that Ben would pay.

Skidmore didn't comprehend the magnitude of the moment. No one in the van ever said, *Holy shit! This is a kidnapping!*

Skidmore had taken Nick's pager and handed it to Hollywood, who was checking it while it was beeping. Hollywood asked Nick, "Is that your brother?"

Nick knew it was his mom. Hollywood panicked. "She's already looking for the kid!"

Jesse Rugge spoke up, asking Hollywood about their next move. Hollywood didn't know. He simply tossed the pager onto the dash and asked Nick to turn over any other things he had in his possession—a small bag of weed, a glass pipe, a wallet with a little phone book, and that Baggie of Valium.

Hollywood also removed Nick's red ruby ring. The ring had been passed down from his grandparents to his father when his father was sixteen years old. Jeff then passed it down to Ben on his birthday. It was Jeff's hope that Ben would one day pass it down to his son. Maybe Ben didn't feel worthy, so he passed it on to Nick on his bar mitzvah.

Nick resisted, yet Hollywood yanked it off. "That's my dad's ring!"

Rugge finally convinced Hollywood to return it.

After his parents divorced when he was eleven, Rugge had split time between his father's house in the Hidden Valley area of Santa Barbara and his mother's in West Hills.

His natural athleticism, lean torso, and height would have had most Division I baseball coaches salivating. But those Saturday mornings of running down fly balls with ease during Little League seemed a century ago. Rugge had done a short stint in jail for DUI instead of paying a fine. At twenty, he was still bouncing between parents. His father taught him to harbor his own hate, which led Rugge to despise him.

Rugge had started selling pot at thirteen years old. He fell in love with the lifestyle of making quick money. It took him down a different path, one that now included smoking weed, taking LSD, and eating mushrooms.

As much as his parents' split informed his unnamed rage,

his warm smile put strangers at ease. His charm was infectious, brotherly, healing.

Instead of taking cuts at bat, he was taking cuts from whatever he sold from marijuana sales. He was Hollywood's northern connection. Now, he was his driver.

Chapter 7

PANIC AT HOME

NICK WAS QUIET IN THE VAN AND DID WHAT HE WAS told. Back home, Susan was going through his drawers, looking for clues that could give her any answers to his disappearance.

It seemed as if it was yesterday that Nick was gathering bugs and placing them inside a plasma ball as a practical joke. Susan wouldn't know what the awful smell was permeating the house. It was Nick, burning bugs. Other times he would place trash cans out in the street or stack chairs so his mother couldn't reach them. Harmless jokes? Could Nick disappearing like this be another one? Susan could only hope. But she knew she wasn't fooling herself either. She said she had always told him, whatever the cause, whatever obstacles he would face, to seek the positive, and to live with happiness no matter the trials or tribulations. Susan couldn't have imagined that being kidnapped fit into an entirely different category of obstacle.

This philosophy had been passed down to her from her father, who was a sign maker. She, in turn, had tried to imprint this same advice in her hazel-eyed son, Nick. Yes, he was young, but his mentality, compassion, and insight exceeded his age. He had an innate ability to find a commonality with anyone. He was so "intuitive," from the very beginning.

Susan had also impressed upon her son never to take the low road and gossip about people. This was another reason Nick was so likable. He would go out of his way to engage others. He could meet someone and connect "instantly." So adaptable, "he made you smile."

Susan felt fortunate that she was blessed with Nick. Jeff was her third husband. After her first marriage dissolved, she married an older man with three children. "I was a full-time step-mom." She still secretly hoped. "All I wanted was a baby. He decided after four years [together] he didn't want any more." But with Jeff, she no longer had to wish. She would give birth at twenty-five years old.

Nicholas Samuel Markowitz was named after Susan's late "favorite sister-in-law's grandfather." He was Italian. "A ninety-six-year-old man who cooked me spaghetti" just prior to her pregnancy. "Such an awesome man with a beautiful name!" It stuck.

Nick was raised Jewish. It was against the religion to be named after someone who was still living, but that didn't stop Susan and Jeff from choosing Nick's middle name after his living grandfather—Jeff's father. His grandfather made an exception.

Fond moments for Susan Markowitz were not just Nick's first concert seeing the Beach Boys or summer camping trips along the Kern River, but seemingly ordinary car rides. It was "our ritual, our private time" where she would take him to school, pick him up, then drive him to his Hebrew classes. She cherished those forty minutes between mother and son that occurred three times a week.

As it was getting later in the day on that August 6, Susan was still trying to page Nick. She waited for his call. She would not receive one.

She would go through his coat pockets and pants for a second and third and fourth time. There had to be a clue. She kept hoping her Little Boy Blue would come home safely. But she knew her son was far removed from that home video of him at nineteen months old. In it, he was dressed in white OshKosh B'gosh overalls pinned over a striped polo, his right hand fastened around a toy horse, a farmer figurine in a yellow hat clasped in the other. He rocked back and forth in a child's chaise lounge, reciting "Little Boy Blue" while his father encouraged him behind the lens of a camcorder:

> Little boy blue,
> Come blow your horn.
> The sheep's in the meadow.
> The cow's in the corn.
> But where is the boy
> Who looks after the sheep?
> He's under a haystack,
> Fast asleep.

Susan wouldn't find any clues. The closest thing she had was the journal that they shared. Susan had started a writing log with Nick a month after his eighth birthday. It was a sanctuary for self-expression where neither mother nor son would judge or be judged.

As easygoing, likable, and convivial as Nick was in the presence of others, he had a private side, sharing his most personal views and emotions within that journal. As a ten-year-old fourth grader, Nick didn't shy away from offering lessons about showing gratitude:

Giving thanks means appreciate [sic] something and telling people you care about them. It also means to thank someone for something they've given or done for you.

He would later conclude:

Because if we're not than [sic] that's what usually . . . starts gangs, and people get killed like that.

By thirteen, he was signing his entries: *Love, Rabbi Nick Markowitz*.

Out of all the shared writing, one entry would haunt Susan. It was the journal entry Nick *didn't* write about where he was going on that Sunday morning.

Chapter 8

ONWARD TO FIESTA (FOR ALL BUT ONE)

VIDEO FROM AUGUST 4, 2000—TWO DAYS BEFORE Nick's abduction—highlighted *charros* in tight-cut trousers and heavily embroidered shirts with sequined outlined roses. They marched down State Street atop Camarillo White Horses. These traditional horsemen from Mexico proudly held the American flag with black gloves that extended along the forearm and matched their bow ties. Behind them, flower girls wore vibrant blooms in their hair that contrasted with their white *china poblana* dresses.

They were taking part in one of the nation's largest equestrian parades, spanning eight decades.

Fiesta, from its inception in August of 1924, prided itself on the city's heritage from the Mexican and Spanish pioneers who first settled here. Events such as Casa Cantina and La Fiesta Pequeña featured songs and dances from flamenco to *folklorico*.

Tours of the Spanish Colonial Revival courthouse were offered over the course of the five-day celebration.

Fiesta was where Hollywood, Jesse Rugge, and William Skidmore were supposed to be headed. They couldn't attend now. Not with Nick in the van. His kidnapping ran counter to the spirit of a festival promoting "friendliness, hospitality, and tolerance."

Skidmore never engaged in conversation with Nick while driving. Rugge and Hollywood were talking about where they could go to just sit and talk. Then Rugge said he knew someone in Santa Barbara.

The van would make a stop to pick up Skidmore's friend Brian Affronti. When twenty-year-old Affronti entered the van, he was in the dark about Nick being kidnapped. No one even introduced him. The only communication would be a glance from Skidmore that told Affronti, *Don't worry about this, it'll be all right.*

Skidmore had known Affronti since the second grade. Affronti used to live down the street from him in Simi Valley. He was the little blue-eyed kid with the eyelashes, who never got in a fight.

Affronti had known Hollywood for six months, introduced through Skidmore. He would buy marijuana off Hollywood to sell on consignment while trying to raise money for a night-club. The way the dope game worked when being fronted marijuana was simple. You would sell what Hollywood supplied at a higher price, then pay him back the original cost, keeping the profit for yourself.

Skidmore's friendship was so strong with Affronti because Affronti's parents enjoyed his company. Skidmore used to go to his house all the time in fourth and fifth grade. It was like a second home, where Skidmore was the big brother. That meant loyalty. That meant never backing down from defending Affronti.

At school, if someone messed with Affronti, Skidmore was going to go talk to him. After Affronti had been beaten up during a fight, Skidmore told his friend, "Watch this," and proceeded to start a fight with the kid who had pestered Affronti. Everyone knew that Skidmore was quicker with his hands and hit a lot harder. Everybody was afraid to fight him.

However, there was no one to fight right now. Hollywood couldn't find Ben, so he had settled on abducting his fifteen-year-old brother.

They made one more stop, at Skidmore's house. He was diabetic and needed his insulin shot, which he didn't have on him.

Twenty-year-old Ryan Hoyt wasn't in the van. Hoyt had been relegated to cleaning up the broken glass at Hollywood's and to finish packing his belongings for the move out. Though over six feet tall and athletic, Hoyt was Hollywood's indentured servant. It appears demeaning himself was the only way Hoyt could stay in Hollywood's good graces. Hoyt would smoke up a twelve-hundred-dollar debt for inhaling more product than he pushed. And that made him an easy mark. Constantly berated, Hoyt never stuck up for himself.

One of Hollywood's pets, a pit bull named Chump, might have been treated better. Hoyt would know. He was tasked with cleaning up after the dog, along with other menial chores—

landscaping, painting, washing cars, even picking up Hollywood's younger brother from school. Sometimes even babysitting. Whatever he could do to work off the debt. He cultivated a new identity by being *stripped* of one.

He would have also been riding in the van during Nick's kidnapping if he didn't have to stay behind and sweep up those busted windows. Hoyt did everything for Hollywood except shade him with an umbrella.

Self-sabotaging garnered Hoyt the attention he wouldn't find from his fractured family. At an early age, Hollywood's was his surrogate one. He was even invited on vacations.

Hoyt's parents divorced when he was five years old. He would always complain to Skidmore about his stepmom and how she was always yelling at him. His dad was cool to his friends. But in the privacy of their home, Hoyt caught the brunt of his father's anger.

Hoyt found validation in all the wrong places. Even if it was the wrong kind. He owed Hollywood money, and Hollywood would rub it in his face and embarrass him in front of his friends.

Burning bridges was less talent than innate quality. Hollywood purchased a car for Hoyt as a birthday gift and threw in tires and registration. Hoyt ended up collecting a grand in parking tickets. However, he had never taken the time to transfer over the registration. Hollywood was on the hook.

Hoyt accrued more weekly interest from his debt than what he made working at a local market. But it was only twelve hundred dollars. It's not like Hollywood would have someone murdered for that amount, right?

The taunting grew. In that same video where Hollywood fronted as a Crip, he demonstrated the requisite stoner art of a slowly exhaled bong rip before turning the camera on Hoyt.

Hollywood pushed him to name the dollar amount he better see the next day.

Like Hollywood's understudy, Hoyt wore his ball cap backward, pulled so low it obscured his eyebrows. "Five hundred," he said, leaning in. Emphatic, but not the least bit convincing.

Hollywood would throw parties and humiliate Hoyt in front of everybody. He was forced to crush empty beer cans, clean out ashtrays, and scrub the counters. Hollywood didn't want Hoyt to wait until *after* the party ended. He wanted Hoyt to do it while it was still raging. Hollywood would take off fifty dollars here and there. But if Hoyt had to buy cleaning supplies, that money was added on to the debt because again, Hollywood was fronting it.

Hollywood was smart in choosing his battles. He'd prey on the weak-minded and leave his other crew members alone, knowing they wouldn't take his insults. No, that would end up in a fistfight Hollywood and his five-foot-four-inch frame didn't stand a chance of winning.

But for all of Hollywood's provocation, Hoyt would continue to swallow it. And instead of heading to Fiesta with the guys, he was once again relegated to maid duty.

That day's occasion would be the first time Affronti attended

Fiesta. It was also the first time he had ever seen Nick Markowitz. He didn't realize this was Ben Markowitz's brother. He and Ben had mutual friends and would see each other at parties. To Affronti, Nick didn't look like he had been beaten up. In fact, Nick was just sitting quietly.

However, Affronti did have an uneasy feeling. Even though Nick wasn't talking, Affronti knew he was there involuntarily. From the front seat, Hollywood kept launching threatening remarks. "If your brother thinks he's going to kill my family, you know, he has another think coming. Your brother is going to pay me my money right now." Affronti quickly put the pieces together. *This is Ben's younger brother!*

Nick would speak only when spoken to. When he was pressed about Ben's whereabouts, he responded that he wasn't sure he knew what Ben did and that Ben didn't live at home. He even asked Hollywood why he was doing this.

There was sporadic joking, but it was always shrouded in tension. Hollywood split up Nick's Valium and weed. Something to cut the mood when the joking wouldn't. Hollywood made it clear to Nick: "If you run, I'll break your teeth." That comment would give Skidmore pause, seeing as he couldn't recall Hollywood settling his own battles. Hollywood paid everyone else to take care of his problems.

Hollywood was still constantly checking Nick's pager. And Nick's mother? Susan couldn't exactly hashtag *findnickmarkowitz*. There was no social media in terms of Facebook, Instagram, or Twitter. The 24/7 news crawl didn't exist.

Fed up, Hollywood tossed the pager and Nick's black phone book onto the side of the road.

Even though the van was headed to Santa Barbara, they would hold their own Fiesta—away from those *charros* and sequined roses on Cabrillo Boulevard and State Street—three miles away on Modoc Road.

Chapter 9

MORE CONFUSION

THE PROPERTY ON MODOC HAD SHARP BLOOMS OF yucca out front. It was a townhome with other small homes around it. Richard Hoeflinger, twenty, lived there. He had been friends with Rugge since elementary. That day, it was a revolving door of Hoeflinger's guests, smoking and drinking, coming and going from the residence. A whole new group of guys would add to those numbers.

However, Hoeflinger wasn't home at the time the white van pulled up around three p.m. His friend Gabriel Ibarra was, smoking out front. After Rugge walked up, Gabriel informed him that Hoeflinger wasn't home yet, so Rugge waited across the street for his friend to return.

Hoeflinger had planned to attend a barbecue close by when he briefly returned and saw Rugge.

Rugge told him he had a few friends who "wanted to come in and kick it." Hoeflinger was just running in and out but said that it would be fine for Rugge and his friends to hang. At some point Nick's wrists were bound with duct tape inside the van.

What happened next was something Hoeflinger wasn't expecting. Nick had a shirt thrown over his hands to hide the fact that his wrists were bound. Hoeflinger's roommate, Hoeflinger's cousin, his cousin's friend, and another friend were also present. Hollywood's crew escorted Nick into a back bedroom. About twenty minutes later Hoeflinger went to check up on them.

Ibarra didn't think anything was wrong when Hollywood's crew went into Hoeflinger's room. But then he saw Hoeflinger come out by himself with a shocked look on his face.

Hoeflinger had seen the tape being removed from Nick's wrists at the same time Nick was being offered a water bong. Hoeflinger threw Skidmore a look: *What are you guys doing with this kid?* He then confided in Skidmore that his guests were tripping out and that Hollywood's crew had to get Nick out of there. And for good reason. Ibarra had also seen into the room, where Nick was bound at the feet and wrists by duct tape and had a sock over his eyes like a temporary blindfold.

Hoeflinger and Ibarra didn't want to cause any trouble after seeing a bulge, which they presumed to be a gun, under Hollywood's shirt. Ibarra then surmised that Nick was being held against his will. Ibarra felt *somebody* had to be armed to be able to pull this kidnapping off.

A short time later, Ibarra watched as Hollywood smoked while pacing out back. Rugge told Ibarra that Hollywood was freaking out because "he took this kid."

Hollywood then walked up to Ibarra and whispered to him, his hand on the bulge in his waistband. "Keep your fucking mouth shut, you don't say nothing."

Hoeflinger had met Hollywood six months earlier at Hollywood's home, where Ryan Hoyt was pointing a Mac-10 in his direction to intimidate him. He had already had one gun pointed in his face. He wanted to do anything he could to avoid repeating the experience. Maybe that was why he accepted a bribe from Hollywood to use his place to hold Nick in the short term.

It wasn't just Hoeflinger who didn't want to be involved. Another friend of Hoeflinger's who was also at his apartment felt that Hollywood was "on a mission," but she also decided not to go to the police.

Hoeflinger's cousin was freaked out when she initially saw Nick duct-taped. That didn't stop her from still using the bathroom in the bedroom to put on her makeup. She also chose not to go to the police, fearing repercussions for anyone involved.

In one version or another, it would be explained to all the witnesses that Nick's brother owed Hollywood money.

Twenty minutes after that white van arrived, Hoeflinger, his cousin, and his cousin's friend left to attend the barbecue. Hollywood was "barking orders" at his crew. Hoeflinger, though frightened, chose not to report the kidnapping to police because he was afraid of Hollywood. He hoped Hollywood would be gone by the time he returned.

At the same time, Ibarra headed to work as the manager-supervisor of Kentucky Fried Chicken. Once there, he didn't tell anyone about what he had just witnessed. He was also fearful and scared. He thought to himself, *If I say something and these guys find out, what will happen if they then come for me?* He felt Hollywood was not right in the head, and that if he had kidnapped Nick, what would stop Hollywood from doing the same to him?

After Hoeflinger and his crew left, Brian Affronti had seen enough. He had seen Nick duct-taped and given a "bong hit." He turned to Skidmore. He wanted out. He had no intention of staying a minute longer. He quickly made up an excuse—he forgot he had a date. Hollywood gave him shit for it, then begrudgingly said he could take the van, but only after Hollywood used it so he could go to Rugge's to shower.

Unlike Affronti, who lied to Hollywood, Skidmore actually did have a date with his girlfriend. Would Skidmore decide to ride this kidnapping out, staying loyal to Hollywood, or would he respect Affronti's request to leave? Just exactly what type of guy was Skidmore?

Years before he would be recognized by his street name, Capone, William Skidmore went by the Blanket, a name given to him in Little League by his coach, Jack Hollywood, whom he played for under the elite Westhills Mustang and Bronco Divisions. William "covered the whole field." He didn't care if he got hurt diving for balls. Hence, the Blanket was born.

For Skidmore, this was the endgame—making a name for yourself. And that name started changing early in the party scene. The Blanket soon faded into a haze of bong hits and acid trips. By sixth grade he was drinking beer and smoking weed. By seventh it was on to cocaine, and by eighth, LSD was the fashionable escape. By ninth grade, he was best friends with the local cocaine dealer. The best place to hang was at a friend's whose parents were divorced. That meant Skidmore and his friends usually had the house to themselves until a parent arrived home from work.

Being cool wasn't enough for Skidmore. He thought that to fit in he would also need to cultivate an intimidation factor. He wanted to prove himself. He wanted to be the *guy*. And that guy joined one of the most notorious and ruthless Asian gangs in the San Fernando Valley. And he would do it *twice*. Same Asian gang, two locations.

Skidmore wasn't Asian, but because his hood was in constant battle with its rival, his gang dropped the race requisite and allowed blacks and whites to join without repercussions.

In eleventh grade, the Blanket gave way to his new hood name, Scrappy, because of his love for fighting. His motto was "Punch first, talk later."

Because he had friends who were affiliated with the gang from Long Beach, he was jumped in to that clique first. But since some of his friends didn't reside in Long Beach, they started their own satellite branch in San Fernando. Hence, why Skidmore was jumped in twice.

Being put on a gang is a rite of passage. There are no interviews or letters of recommendation. No, your résumé is written *for you* in right hooks and how well you handle the fusillade of fists for sixty seconds, courtesy of current members. He was jumped in by eight members the first time around. The second time, it was seven.

Scrappy finally stepped aside for Capone. It wasn't after the infamous gangster as some members of law enforcement assumed. *Capone* means "brown" in Tagalog, which some of his Filipino crew used in tribute to Skidmore being part Mexican.

Skidmore held his first gun at age fifteen. He acquired it during the summer of 1995, when he used to rob houses. *Ten a day.* That was where he would find a new gun every month.

He was first incarcerated at age seventeen in Barry J. Nidorf Juvenile Hall in Sylmar, California, about forty minutes northeast of West Hills. He was being prosecuted for more than twenty-four residential burglaries. He spent ten months fighting his case. There was one witness, a housekeeper who saw him climb through a window into a residence. When they made eye contact, he jumped out and ran. He was with two other friends. The housekeeper, who was the only witness, never showed. She was from Guatemala and didn't have a green card. Fearing deportation, she never testified. The judge threw out the case.

Skidmore had *SFV*—San Fernando Valley—tattooed across his chest. It was commissioned at age sixteen. He was Hollywood's muscle and never sold marijuana. He was Hollywood's friend "who was from a gang." And if Hollywood had an issue with someone,

Skidmore would take care of it. That was what Hollywood did—he paid everyone to take care of his problems.

Skidmore decided that things were getting too heavy at Hoeflinger's, that this kidnapping might not be over anytime soon. After all, Hollywood still hadn't made an attempt to contact Ben Markowitz, even though he was busy making phone calls on Hoeflinger's phone. Who was he speaking to? Had the situation now reached the point of no return? Was Hollywood compartmentalizing the information or his plan, delegating on a need-to-know or reaching out to outside sources for their input? No. He was looking for a separate ride home.

This entire time, Susan Markowitz was still frantically paging Nick, having no idea where her son was or that his pager had been tossed on the side of the 101 freeway. She spent her nervous energy cleaning his room.

Skidmore agreed with Affronti that things were getting out of hand. Even though he smoked a bong with Nick and drank Tanqueray, the mood was anything but festive. Skidmore would express his concerns to Affronti. "Dude, this is crazy, fuck man." He thought, *If Ben hadn't broken out those windows, none of this would have happened.* "That was the spark," he said, "that lit the fuse." And now Skidmore was wrapped up in something he desperately wanted to distance himself from.

Hollywood finally left for Rugge's. Nick remained. Affronti and Skidmore could have freed him. But instead they anxiously waited for Hollywood to return. They wanted out.

Affronti knew one thing: there was no chance he was going to the police. He felt that if he said something to Hollywood about kidnapping Nick, or turned to the authorities, Jesse could come back for him. Affronti reasoned, *He's already done this to somebody that his crew didn't have a problem with*. Affronti didn't know if Hollywood would turn around and do the same to him if he expressed his opinion that they should let Nick go.

When the van returned, Skidmore and Affronti left Hoeflinger's. That was when Affronti realized he'd forgotten his cell phone. When they returned to Hoeflinger's to pick it up, Nick was untied. In fact, he was smoking weed and playing video games with Rugge. This time, Hollywood was nowhere to be found. He had gotten a separate ride back home to West Hills.

Was this the point when Nick went from feeling helpless to feeling empowered by his abduction? Was his rationale, *Fuck it, let's just ride this sucker out*? Did he get a rush from believing his capture was more alluring than alarming?

Four hours later, around seven p.m., Hoeflinger returned from the barbecue. Rugge and Nick were still playing video games. At least Nick wasn't tied up. Hoeflinger might have felt a small sense of relief.

The same couldn't be said for Susan Markowitz, still frantically paging her son.

Chapter 10

BUYING TIME

NORMALLY, IT TOOK APPROXIMATELY THIRTY-THREE minutes to walk the 1.7 miles from Modoc Road to 780 Casiano Drive. But running on Tanqueray and bong hits? That added considerable time. Rugge had nowhere else to take Nick. And Hollywood? Was nowhere to be found.

It was now Rugge's job to watch Nick, something he wasn't too pleased about having to do. Why didn't Hollywood take Nick back to Los Angeles? Ben was the one with whom he had issues. Out of options, Rugge and Nick headed out from Richard Hoeflinger's apartment to Rugge's father's house in the Hidden Valley area of Santa Barbara.

When Rugge and Nick finally made it to Jesse Rugge's house, they entered to cigarette smoke wafting from the kitchen. Jesse introduced Nick to his father, his stepmother, and a family friend. Nick was just a friend visiting from Los Angeles who was going to spend the night.

Rugge grabbed a beer and even offered one to Nick. They watched some TV. He gave Nick some options—his bed, the floor, or the couch downstairs. Nick took the floor. Jesse provided blankets and a pillow.

Back at the Markowitzes', Susan had also grabbed a pillow—Nick's. Her mind racing a million miles per hour, she tried to make sense of where he could have gone and why he hadn't contacted her. In the past, he had always let her know where he was, or Ben would call to let her know that Nick was with him. Ben would let Nick spend the night, then take him home in the morning. Was he safe? Where was he sleeping? Was he hurt? It seemed like yesterday that she was singing Nick to sleep as a small boy.

Not only did Susan conclude her journal entries to Nick with, *I love you so much*. This phrase was also the name of a 1984 children's song by Barbara Milne:

> *I love you so much, I love you so much*
> *I can't even tell you how much I love you . . .*

And when she wasn't singing, she was reading to Nick: *Once there was a tree . . . and she loved a little boy*. This was a line from Shel Silverstein's *The Giving Tree*. Out of the six hundred books in her library, two hundred belonged to Nick.

Forget baseball, where he broke his wrist at age seven after being pinged by a wild pitch. His favorite pastime was reading. And before he could read, Susan would play cassettes and let him listen to stories or Gymboree music as he fell asleep.

Susan pored over the journal again. They had a system to writing new entries. When he was ready to share, he would place the journal on her pillow. She would then follow up and place it on his. There was never any pressure to write, because she didn't want it to seem like more homework.

Had Nick made a whole new set of friends she hadn't known about? Occasionally Jeff Markowitz would add his own thoughts to the journal. In one entry he encouraged his son to make the right decisions:

> In the future, be sure you think of the consequences of
> your actions before you decide to do things. One thing you
> have to be very careful of in your life is not to let anybody
> convince you to do something you don't feel is right. Be
> good, I love you, Dad. PS—next week will be better.

Susan left one last voice mail for Nick before trying to get some sleep. Even though he was missing and she was upset, she didn't berate him. "Nick, it's Mom. Call me back. I love you." Every time she called, she would leave the same message and express her love.

But tonight, there was no Nick. Or singing or reading. Just his pillow tightly clasped in a worried mother's arms.

* * *

As much as Susan worried about her son's disappearance, Nick's close friend Carey Evans wasn't as concerned.

Carey, who was a year older, met Nick in art class during his junior year and Nick's sophomore year of high school. Their friendship started off like most high school friendships do: they sat next to each other and found out they had some friends in common, and that they could easily make the other laugh.

For Carey, it was the first time that he had started up a friendship with a random person. Up until then, he had made most of his friends through sports, family friendships, or other classes he had attended with them for many years.

Carey and Nick had sparked a closer friendship during the summer. They were two teenagers without much to do, spending most days just killing time, testing the limits of their boundaries in what Carey described as "a pretty boring, suburban part of the Valley."

They were sometimes up to no good, but it was "never serious: loitering, small-time vandalism, smoking cigarettes and some pot here and there."

Carey thought Nick was "trying to grow into an image that he had of himself as a bit of the 'cool guy'—in a James Dean, *Rebel Without a Cause* type of way." For Carey, "it was that time of life when you try to be who you think you want to be, rather than who you *actually* are." They hadn't yet realized it wasn't worth the trouble trying to be someone you're not.

Carey and Nick never spoke much about dreams or girls. This

was the summer before Nick was to turn sixteen, and they were "full of late-teenage angst—more concerned with looking cool in front of each other than really sharing any type of deep emotions."

It wasn't a big deal when Carey found out Nick was missing. Carey—like everyone—thought he had just run away for a little bit. "Not run away in the real sense that some people run away from really difficult home situations as kids—more the run away in the teenage drama-queen sense, where you go stay with some friends you have that your parents don't know about."

Carey knew that Nick always bragged that he had older friends—mostly through Ben, so it "kind of made the whole running away for a couple days a bit less alarming." Carey mostly thought, *Man, he's going to be in trouble when he gets back*. Not, *I hope he's safe and okay*.

Rugge and Nick were falling asleep in Rugge's room with the television on. Did either wish that this odyssey would all be over? Was Rugge more annoyed than frightened? Did he look at this fifteen-year-old and wonder if his parents were scared shitless? What kept him from picking up the phone and calling them, or anyone? Like Skidmore's thinking, this was all just supposed to blow over. Ben Markowitz would be found. Things would be squared. Nick would be returned. Easy, right?

Rugge and Nick would wake the next morning as if nothing was out of the ordinary. Rugge would sweep one part of the house, Nick, the other. A friend would stop by. But he was more than a friend. He was the great-grandson of the founder of Old Spanish Days. His name was Graham Pressley, and he was about to be enveloped in something more than just a casual summer-morning hang, something that would lead to the foothills above Goleta and Lizard's Mouth.

Chapter 11

WITNESSES

NATASHA ADAMS WAS A SEVENTEEN-YEAR-OLD working at Riley's Flowers and attending Santa Barbara City College. She lived in the lower Riviera section of Santa Barbara.

That Monday, August 7, 2000, she was with three friends, Jesse Rugge, Graham Pressley, age seventeen, and Kelly Carpenter, sixteen, at Rugge's father's home. They were close to being an everyday quartet. Today, though, there was someone new she had never seen or met before—a fifteen-year-old with scrapes on his elbow, Nicholas Markowitz.

Curious, she asked him how old he was and where he went to high school. They talked music and skateboarding. Nick told her he liked to do tae kwon do, even though he wasn't very good at it. To Kelly, Nick was very sweet and friendly. He *seemed* calm like everyone else.

However, Natasha was skeptical. She came to the conclusion

that something was wrong. She asked Pressley about Nick. Her worst fears were confirmed. Nick had been kidnapped. And not only kidnapped, he was asked to vacuum the floor. Things didn't make sense. This was not like Rugge. He was known to be generous and hospitable, never asking his friends to do anything for him. It was out of character.

Natasha wondered why Rugge told them not to allow Nick to use the phone. She didn't ask Rugge directly but instead confided in Pressley. He disclosed that the kidnapping had happened when Rugge went down to Los Angeles to meet up with Jesse Hollywood. Nick was collateral when they couldn't find Ben Markowitz.

Pressley wasn't worried at first. Rugge had told him that Nick was just going to stay for a couple of days and by all means, make him feel at home.

Kelly found out the real reason Nick was there when Natasha leaned over out of earshot of Nick, who was sitting across the table from them. *Nick had been kidnapped*. Even after Natasha informed her, Kelly still thought the entire situation was surreal. "There wasn't anything to enforce a seriousness in the situation."

Even though Natasha was concerned that Nick was being held against his will, the whole scenario didn't seem real. Everyone was friendly, and the atmosphere wasn't tense at all. "It was mostly light and like, fun." They were watching television, smoking cigarettes and weed. Nick confided to Natasha that he was addicted to Valium. Did he think this would somehow impress her? He told her he was seventeen. Maybe bumping up his age would do it? He then confided he was a couple of years younger.

Later in the day on that Monday, August 7, Natasha would drive herself, Kelly, Nick, Rugge, and Pressley back to her house. When she went upstairs to use the bathroom, Rugge had already left. He had a meeting with Hollywood, who had driven up.

At her house, Natasha never offered Nick the use of the phone. Why would she wait for him to ask? Nick made the decision for her. He told her "that it was okay because he was doing it for his brother, and that as long as his brother was okay, he was okay." This put her at ease.

Nick wasn't going anywhere. He was going along for the ride. He didn't want to stir the waters for his brother. For Nick, Ben had been through enough. He loved his brother and didn't want to add to his troubles. No, Nick, in fact, wanted to try to be a part of the solution. Even if it meant being held against his will. Even if it was under the guise of just riding it out.

Nick asked Natasha for some rubbing alcohol and Neosporin to clean the scrape on his elbow. He mentioned that Hollywood was looking for his brother but never told her why. Pressley would let her know the reason.

At this point, this was the only time Nick was *not* with his original kidnappers.

Hollywood had driven with his girlfriend to Santa Barbara at Rugge's request. They headed to East Beach to grab lunch. Rugge didn't eat, pressing Hollywood about taking Nick home. Hollywood just shrugged and changed the subject. Rugge was growing agitated. This wasn't his problem or mess. But it was just like Hollywood to be unable to fight his own battles.

Rugge called Natasha and told her to bring Nick back to his house. She drove back with Kelly and Pressley. She had yet to vocalize her concern to Rugge that what he was a part of wasn't a good idea. She was still in shock and trying to process everything. She kept telling herself that it wasn't a big deal. Nick *appeared* to be going along with it. Anytime she thought about doing something, she talked herself down. *I don't want to be involved!*

Two other guests had come over to Rugge's. Hollywood and his girlfriend, Michelle Lasher. Natasha was concerned when she saw Hollywood. She didn't trust him. Or his bad energy.

Hollywood walked into the living room where everyone was sitting. Natasha looked over his girlfriend. They had never met. Lasher was five foot three with seemingly fake breasts. She had French-manicured toenails and fingernails and was super skinny. She was wearing jeans, white-heeled shoes, and a shirt that exposed her navel.

Natasha watched as Lasher propped herself on Hollywood's lap. Seeing new faces didn't keep Hollywood and Lasher from being affectionate.

However, for Nick, there was a negative physiological reaction when Hollywood entered the living room, so much that he didn't speak when he excused himself and headed upstairs.

Hollywood only stayed for about thirty minutes. Natasha no longer wanted to hang out with Hollywood. She heard parts of a conversation where Hollywood mentioned "baseball bat." She wondered if this was in reference to hurting Nick. She threw him a sharp look.

When discussing plans for the night, Kelly couldn't tell if Hollywood was serious or joking when he told the group, "We'll just tie the kid up and toss him in the back of the car and go get dinner and go swimming at the Fess Parker or the Biltmore or something." Nick didn't hear this conversation. He was still upstairs in Rugge's room.

Nick would come to be referred to as the "Stolen Boy."

On Tuesday, August 8, *forty-eight hours* into Nick's abduction, Natasha expressed her concern to Pressley. She was the only one with a car, so she didn't mind driving to pick him up. From there, they headed to Rugge's where Kelly met them.

Natasha had become worried about the situation. *What was Nick still doing there?* Hollywood had come and gone and didn't take Nick with him. Rugge was becoming more stressed, feeling like the official babysitter.

While at Rugge's Natasha went for a walk with Pressley and Kelly. She wanted to ask Pressley privately if Nick was going to be killed. He was taken aback. He told her, "Of course not." But then he confided a darker secret: Hollywood had offered Rugge two thousand dollars to kill Nick. Rugge declined it. Once again, William Skidmore was right—Hollywood was known to pay everyone else to do his bidding.

Natasha kept a secret of her own. She didn't tell Pressley that on the previous night she had turned to her mother, who was an attorney, for advice. Natasha wanted to know about the charges for kidnapping, speaking vaguely when referencing the situation. She had told her mother it involved some kids she knew and a boy who had been kidnapped. Her mother was shocked. *Kids kidnapping kids?*

Natasha's mother advised her to go to the police. She did not, hoping the situation would blow over. She was also in fear of retaliation by Hollywood if he found out. If it came down to saying anything, even if it was a question of whether Nick's life was in danger, she could lie to herself.

Pressley—a local pot dealer under Rugge—remained concerned. He was helpless and didn't know what to do. He advised Natasha not to say a thing. He didn't want anyone going to jail. He also told her they could possibly end up dead because Jesse Hollywood was crazy. When Pressley and Kelly headed inside Rugge's, Natasha stayed behind to compose herself. She was still crying and wanted to calm herself.

Kelly confided to Nick how upset Natasha had become. "Why?" Nick said. "Is it because of me?" He told her, "Don't worry about it, it's just another story to tell my grandkids."

Natasha finally went inside. She would speak to Rugge in his dining room. When Rugge told her that she looked like she had been crying, Natasha replied that she was worried about Nick's well-being. What were they going to do with him? She made Rugge promise that they were going to take Nick home. Rugge made the promise. He looked her in the eyes and swore to her he was going to take Nick home. Or at least put him on a Greyhound bus.

Natasha didn't confront Rugge about the fact that she had

been told about Hollywood's offer for him to kill Nick. No matter what the outcome, she just didn't want to be involved.

Rugge had had enough. Why hadn't Hollywood taken Nick home yet?

Rugge constantly paced, then sat down and told Kelly that he didn't want "to be in a situation." In front of everyone, he told Nick, "I don't think that I should be a part of this, and I'm going to get you home. I'm going to give you fifty dollars. You're taking a train home tonight, and then you'll have some money left over to get a cab home." The one thing he didn't want to have happen was for the police to arrive at his home the next day and question him.

Rugge asked Nick how he could be sure that Nick wouldn't speak about any of the details surrounding his disappearance. Nick put him at ease. "I'm not doing anything now, I'm going along with it, I'm not going to tell anybody. You guys have been nice to me."

To cut the mood, Rugge suggested that they party at a hotel that night. It had been stressful enough. Nick went along with it, never causing waves, remembering he was doing this for his brother.

Then around five thirty p.m. on the evening of August 8, the group headed to the Lemon Tree Inn.

Chapter 12

THE MENTOR

THERE WOULD BE NO PARTYING FOR THE MARKO-
witzes on August 8. They had waited a day and a half, hoping Nick
was at a friend's, or someplace maybe Ben knew. Susan wouldn't
write in the journal she shared with Nick that day. No, the only
writing she would be doing incorporated a spreadsheet with
hundreds of names. It didn't matter if they were close friends,
neighbors, teachers, acquaintances, friends of Ben, or friends of
friends of someone they had never met. She was trying to contact everyone. And yes, *still paging the hell out of her son.*

Jeff Markowitz had filed a missing persons report and taken
out his motorcycle, looking for his son on the trails he used to
ride with Nick. Ben Markowitz hadn't heard from Nick either.
He had been away in Arizona, working a construction job with an
uncle and showed up at their house the previous day, August 7.

Susan couldn't help but wonder what kind of trouble Nick

might be in. He was no angel; he had been in trouble before and things always worked out. He did have other guidance, from Kirk Miyashiro, the dean of students at El Camino Real High School.

Kirk had many arrows in his quiver. Not only was he a reserve police sergeant for Monterey Park, but also a part of the Crime Impact Team that focused on gang activities in the San Gabriel Valley.

There were thirty-eight hundred students divided between Kirk and his two colleagues, each carrying a caseload of around thirteen hundred students. Nick fell under Kirk's supervision for no other reason than where his last name landed alphabetically.

Kirk spent his first ten years in Hawaii, until his family relocated to the Bay Area. He moved down to Southern California, where he received his teaching credential at Long Beach State. From there, he entered the Los Angeles Unified School District as a student teacher. Eighteen years later—which included teaching physical education, health, and biology in middle school—he accepted his position at El Camino.

El Camino was *the* best high school in the LAUSD. The school held four academic decathlon national titles. That spoke volumes of all one hundred and fifty teachers.

Of the school's thirty-eight hundred students, 50 percent came from the local area in the Valley, while the other 50 percent comprised two different arenas. One was called PWT—Permit with Transportation. Those were students who wanted to come out of the inner city—South Central LA and parts of downtown

LA. They all bordered the Compton area. They came to El Camino with permission and transportation provided. That was about 25 percent of the population. The other 25 percent was called CAP. These were students whose schools in the inner city were now at capacity and could no longer take any more students. Those students were reassigned to available schools.

Kirk spent six periods a day doing discipline. He also ran a lunch detention during the day and supervision at night, along with additional supervision for athletic endeavors.

When addressing forms of discipline once a teacher referred a student, the deans had a rubric to follow as to what could be deemed warnings, detentions, Saturday school, suspensions, or expulsions.

Nick Markowitz was one student who fell under this rubric. Kirk had met Nick in ninth grade. Nick was a typical freshman who "got himself in little bits of trouble here and there. Disruptions, nothing serious." Their conversations were always simple and straightforward, without a trace of indignation on Nick's part. "Hey, do you know why you're here?" Nick would own up and they'd move past the issue.

Kirk became more familiar with Nick in the tenth grade. They'd often discuss baseball. His sophomore year an infraction occurred outside the scope of a simple Saturday detention. It fell under trespassing and didn't involve any drugs or weapons. Kirk ended up sending him to another school for ten weeks. The official term was Opportunity Transfer (OT).

Kirk met with Nick and Susan. He told Nick, "Look, you need

a new start, a fresh start. And so what I'm going to do, I'm going to send you to a particular high school in LA in the Valley, so you won't have to go too far." Kirk believed Nick needed some "breathing room."

Nick's demeanor with Kirk was always one of respect. As a dean, Kirk dealt with all kinds of kids, especially those who were always in total denial—*I didn't do that!* Nick was the total opposite. Kirk felt Nick was one of those kids he really needed to save. Nick had made a mistake. But Kirk knew everyone made mistakes. Could Kirk have OT'd him for twenty weeks? Absolutely. He could have OT'd him for the entire year. But Kirk sensed that with his upbringing and polite manners, he would be fine. Kirk's wisdom ran deep like the ancient philosophers: *What an elder sees sitting, the young can't see standing.*

Kirk assured Nick and his parents that he would stay in contact with Nick's dean at his new school, and if he got a good report, he would be welcomed back with open arms. Kirk kept tabs on all his students that he had to OT. He encouraged Nick, "It's only for x number of weeks. Keep your nose clean; I'll check to see where you are." Nick did not raise any protest. He accepted accountability and the temporary transfer.

When it came to dealing with students in trouble, Kirk was a believer in second chances. "I always tried to discipline with a redemptive piece. That's the way I was trained. Yes, we have to lay the hammer down, but there's always ways to come back."

As a reserve officer and dean, Kirk was aware of the underground drug culture. There wasn't a school in the United States that was immune to it. For Kirk, he had to answer the questions, At what level are we affected by it? Is it at El Camino? Absolutely. Could Kirk stop it? He did his best. But with one campus police officer, three deans, and a narc for thirty-eight hundred students? You do the math.

Dealing with the Asian gang culture, Kirk was familiar with the gang William Skidmore was jumped into, though he had never met Skidmore.

As dean at El Camino, he didn't have to traverse the city streets to investigate. No, some gang members were now under the same roof. They came to him. Now he was dealing with crossover not only from Asian and Chicano gangs, but Persian and Aryan Nation gangs as well.

One of his first expulsions during his first month at El Camino involved a CAP student who had gotten into a fight. The student ended up with a loaded gun in the front pocket of his backpack.

It wasn't uncommon for other CAP students to bring their affiliation into the school setting, then mix with locals affiliated with Persian or white Aryan race gangs. One such affiliation was with a particular Aryan brotherhood Ben Markowitz was allegedly associated with at one point. Tattoos of swastikas, lightning bolts, or a woodpecker connoted the affiliation. It seemed it was six degrees of separation in the city of West Hills.

Kirk did his best to intuit potentially dangerous situations. He invested effort to breach systematic and parental failures that stemmed either from gross negligence or a simple lack of awareness.

This would lead him to encourage Nick that much harder. Kirk would have countless one-on-one discussions. He wanted every student to "never be afraid to ask for help."

Kirk wasn't hesitant to intercede with Nick. He knew how much Nick's parents loved him and wanted the best for him. He always believed that education was a partnership. That meant incorporating parents or guardians. However, he knew his influence was limited. The foundational piece came from home. It didn't come from him. He was "an auxiliary." It didn't stop him from having an open door policy for students who didn't have anyone to confide in.

Kirk never wanted to be that individual who had to ask himself, *Why didn't I get involved?* No matter how much defensiveness he encountered from parents, he always had his students' best interests at heart.

That included Nick. "He was never disrespectful to me, took his punishment, and did what he was supposed to do when I asked him to do it." Kirk couldn't ask any more of a student. Nick had Kirk's full respect.

But Nick was now in a situation in which Kirk couldn't intervene. It wasn't Nick this time who'd caused the trouble. Somehow he'd found himself in the middle of it.

Chapter 13

SEEKING ADVICE

WHILE THE GROUP WAS HANGING OUT AT RUGGE'S house, Hollywood went to see his lawyer, Stephen Hogg.

Hogg had litigated Jesse Hollywood out of a couple of previous binds—possession of alcohol as a minor and resisting arrest. Now, the man with a graying ponytail and beard was watching Jesse Hollywood pace and chain-smoke in the backyard of his Simi Valley home. The conversation couldn't have been further from discussing the latest misdemeanor. Hollywood wanted to ascertain the penalty for friends who had kidnapped someone.

Hogg told him it could be life in prison if they asked for ransom. He encouraged Hollywood to contact the authorities and report the incident. Hogg, maybe sensing that Hollywood wasn't being completely forthright with his involvement, advised him that if he stayed ahead of the situation and was the first to report it, maybe the cops would go easier on him. But Hollywood refused. He wouldn't turn himself in. He wouldn't give names. He stormed out.

The situation had reached critical mass. It might have been that Hollywood had already made up his mind about what to do with Nick.

Hollywood was about to graduate from the virtual ranks of PlayStation to actual shot caller with zero interest in rebooting lives. And fuck it if Nick Markowitz was in the wrong place at the wrong time—his role was about to transform from innocent bystander to cautionary tale for anyone who dared to cross this local cannabis dealer.

Hollywood phoned another dealer, Eddy Bachman. He was considered a friend and was never seen as a rival in Hollywood's eyes. Eddy kept pounds of drugs in his car, ready at all times, because there was always someone who wanted to buy. Because there was so much business, the two groups of dealers never messed with each other.

Eddy knew the Markowitz family. He also knew Hollywood's group of friends. They all partied together. Eddy knew Jack Hollywood "had gotten the good stuff for Jesse and his friends to sell." He also knew that Ben didn't owe Hollywood a mere twelve hundred dollars. It was way more. In Eddy's eyes, you didn't kill someone over twelve hundred dollars. You could, however, kill someone if it was thirty-six thousand.

Hollywood had confided in Eddy how Ben owed him money. Hollywood was always trying to play like he was the kingpin. This time he had had enough. *I'm gonna send them a message. You can't just not pay me over and over again and expect me to sit back and let it happen.*

Sometime after Nick's kidnapping, Eddy had encountered Ben Markowitz at TGI Fridays. Ben, who had returned from Arizona, had come in "all jacked up," and blamed it on Eddy and his crew. He thought maybe it was Eddy who had done something to his brother. However, Ben owed everybody money, so he didn't know who might have been behind Nick disappearing.

Eddy had told Ben, "I don't even know your brother. I haven't seen him." Then Ben left. Eddy knew one absolute—*everybody* knew Hollywood had him. Hollywood had told everybody, *I have to send a message.* He kept repeating that to Eddy on the phone. *I'm gonna kill that kid. You don't pay me my money, see what happens.* Eddy didn't believe him. He knew Jesse liked to talk like he was tougher than he was.

Whether Ben's debt was twelve hundred, twenty-four thousand, or thirty-six thousand dollars, as others claimed, Hollywood's "bookkeeping" wasn't something you could exactly audit.

One thing that could be kept track of: Hollywood's TEC-9, which would soon be put to use.

Chapter 14

WHERE IS HOLLYWOOD?

THE LEMON TREE INN WAS RANDOMLY CHOSEN.
Someplace to go—*like a way station for the abducted*—until someone showed up at last and took Nick home. At least that was
everyone's belief.

It was Pressley's mother, Christina, who had given Nick, Kelly,
Jesse Rugge, and her son a ride to the inn. Christina was uneasy,
preoccupied, but it wasn't with the new face she'd never seen. It
was with Jesse Rugge, who she viewed with suspicion because of
his tattoos and influence over her son. She said a quick hello to
Nick, thought he was nice, and that was it.

Natasha would pick up her father from work on Tuesday,
never mentioning Nick or anything about a kidnapping. By the
time she arrived at the Lemon Tree, Jesse Rugge had booked a
room.

***

It was six thirty p.m. in room 341. Everyone drank or smoked. It was Rum and Coke, weed and cigarettes. Nick and Pressley went swimming. Nick ate his final meal—a cheeseburger and fries—though Jesse Hollywood and Ryan Hoyt were the only ones who knew it at the time.

All indications led Natasha to believe that Nick was headed home. Nick appeared to welcome the news. "He seemed happy," Natasha thought. Nick spoke of the music he liked but was more eager to address another topic. When Natasha spoke to him about it, he said when he got home he was going to call his ex-girlfriend. The ex he was referring to was a girl named Jeannie.

Nick had taken Jeannie to the Italian restaurant Alessio's on their first date.

He was thirteen; Jeannie, a year older. Susan, who drove them, had playfully teased her, calling her a "cougar" because of the one-year age difference.

Nick had liked Jeannie for four years. And even though he was almost an hour and a half drive from home, he couldn't wait to express his feelings in the hopes of getting back together with her. Susan believed that Jeannie could very well have been her future daughter-in-law. But Nick wasn't back home yet, and he was what seemed like light-years away from that first date. He wanted to get back and do whatever it took to make things right.

His current situation, though, required him to stay put. That was why he never made a move to leave. Kelly had even asked him why didn't he just get up and walk out of there. Nick, again, said he didn't want to complicate things. "I've taken self-defense and stuff, it's not like I couldn't do anything right now, I just don't want to. I don't see a reason to [stir things up], I'm going home."

Rugge had left for a short period to call Hollywood. At around eleven p.m., he told everyone, except Pressley and Nick, that it was time to go: someone was coming to take Nick home. Natasha left Nick with the parting words, "Have fun. I'm glad you're going home."

Was Rugge now aware of Hollywood and Hoyt's plan? Why would he have Pressley also stay?

Natasha arrived home and slept, confident everything was going to be okay. The same couldn't be said for Rugge. That was because he was anticipating the next knock on room 341 to be from Hollywood. However, Hollywood had other plans that night. He headed over to his girlfriend's place.

Nick fell asleep for some time. Everything seemed normal. That would all change. One more person would be heading up to the Lemon Tree to deal with Nick. It was none other than the twenty-year-old who crushed Hollywood's beer cans and cleaned his ashtrays: Ryan Hoyt. Hoyt wouldn't come empty-handed. He would have Hollywood's TEC-9 in his possession.

Chapter 15

THE ORDER

THE TEC-9 WAS BANNED IN 1994 BY THE CLINTON administration under the Assault Weapons Ban.

The top half of the gun was composed of tube steel. It was parkerized, meaning a chemical coating had been applied to protect against rusting. Its crude sights were stamped sheet metal with a polymer lower receiver. The receiver was a part of the firearm and contained the serial number.

If the user fired from the hip, he would most likely walk it up the target due to the gun's recoil or kickback. "Walk it up" means the gun's user doesn't have complete control of the weapon and that the force from firing it causes the gun to jerk in an upward motion. The holes at the end of the gun, called a barrel shroud, protected the operator from burning his hand. A threaded barrel was another accessory. The one Hoyt was carrying had tape around the handle to make it harder for fingerprints to be lifted. The trigger was also illegally shaved down.

Hollywood had once taken this TEC-9 to a firing range. An employee had noticed it and mentioned he could be hit with jail time for being in possession. The employee never reported it.

Hollywood considered the gun a "throwaway weapon," something to use in case he needed it, a gun that could quickly be discarded. Maybe this was on Ryan Hoyt's mind while he was driving to the Lemon Tree.

And the vehicle Hoyt was driving? Hollywood had turned to Casey Sheehan, a friend he grew up playing baseball with and had known since they were seven years old. Hollywood had inquired whether he could borrow Sheehan's maroon Honda Civic. Sheehan assumed it was for moving. Instead it was Hoyt's transportation to the Lemon Tree.

Hoyt had been sent to the location by Jesse Hollywood as a way to "erase" his debt. Hollywood told him he needed to take care of somebody. But Hollywood didn't refer to Nick by name. No, he depersonalized him, considering Nick a mere nuisance. "There's a *mess* that needs to be cleaned up."

During the last four hours, Hollywood's father, Jack, serendipitously contacted Stephen Hogg regarding a separate issue involving a DUI case in Ventura North.

Jack Hollywood was with his wife, Laurie, close to six hours away up north at a spa, the Ventana, in Big Sur. Stephen Hogg told Jack that Jesse had come to see him earlier in the day. Hogg then got in touch with John Roberts. It was Roberts's white paneled van without windows that Hollywood had used to first kidnap Nick.

John Roberts, who was informed of the kidnapping by Hogg, wanted to find "the boy" and pay him not to say anything about being kidnapped. But then he asked his own rhetorical question: What fifteen-year-old doesn't talk? So instead of calling police, John Roberts had his vehicle scrubbed with solvent to rid it of all evidence.

Back at the Lemon Tree, Nick Markowitz was already asleep when there was a knock on the door. However, when Rugge opened it, it wasn't Hollywood. Instead it was Hoyt. Rugge was annoyed and deflated.

Pressley had never met Hoyt, who quickly made his way to the bathroom with the blue duffel bag. Pressley peered inside and saw Hoyt cleaning a twelve-inch bullet clip that belonged to Hollywood's TEC-9.

The weapon was already considered "dirty," having been used in other crimes. It explained why the gun's origin went all the way to Mesa, Arizona. And now it had found its way to a bathroom at the Lemon Tree Inn, being cleaned by Ryan James Hoyt at 11:20 p.m. on a Tuesday night.

The TEC-9 in general had been involved in close to four thousand cases between 1995 and 1999. This one was about to physically appear *at* the crime scene. Its clip was factory designed to hold up to thirty-five cartridges, but because of weakened springs, the operator could shove an extra two nine-millimeter cartridges into it.

Hoyt was surprised that Graham Pressley was there. He wasn't supposed to be a part of the plan. Hoyt then asked Jesse Rugge why Nick wasn't tied up.

Hoyt told Rugge they were going to his house to pick up shovels. Rugge was scared. He didn't think this was real. He thought Hoyt had lost his mind.

They drove off in Sheehan's car, leaving Pressley alone with Nick. Rugge noticed the TEC-9 tucked into Hoyt's belt. He knew there was no talking Hoyt out of it at this point.

Rugge refused to get the shovels from his house, so Hoyt left him in the car and retrieved them himself.

They returned to the Lemon Tree. Hoyt wanted Rugge to show him a spot to dig a grave. Rugge didn't know the area, so Hoyt had Pressley accompany him, the TEC-9 in plain sight. Rugge stayed behind with Nick.

Hoyt drove thirty minutes north in Casey Sheehan's borrowed car to Lizard's Mouth. After a twenty-minute hike with those shovels in their possession, they decided on what appeared to be an isolated spot.

Hoyt threatened him, "You better start digging if you know what's good for you." Pressley thought he was digging his own grave. He said Hoyt was pointing the now fully loaded automatic right at him.

Pressley dug for about twenty minutes into the sandy

ground, a "grave seven foot by . . . two or three feet, and not very deep."

They then drove back to the Lemon Tree.

At this point on August 8, Susan Markowitz was no longer sleeping on the side of the bed closest to the window so she could hear when Nick walked up and opened their front door. Now she was downstairs on the couch, his pillow clutched between her arms.

Chapter 16

NO GOING BACK

NICK WAS SHAKEN AWAKE. HE WAS LED TO THE CAR and—along with Rugge, Ryan Hoyt, and Graham Pressley—headed to Lizard's Mouth.

Pressley walked with them, approximately twenty feet into the trailhead, showing them which direction to go. He then decided he wanted nothing more to do with what was about to happen. He knew that grave wasn't for him. It was for Nick. He walked back to the car.

Rugge and Hoyt continued on with Nick. Surprisingly at this late hour, hikers passed them on their way down the trail. No conversation took place. The terrain was uneven. One wrong step could end in a sprained ankle. At this time of night, the forlorn landscape appeared ominous and less inviting than it did during the day. As they wound around the trailhead, it became apparent that there was no place to run. Even if Nick decided to flee, he would easily become lost in a labyrinth of boulders, trails, and manzanita trees. He would also have to navigate his way in total darkness. For someone in a disoriented state, it could have become a guessing game. *Am I heading toward the ocean or the road?*

> Little boy blue,
> Come blow your horn.
> The sheep's in the meadow.
> The cow's in the corn.

What was going through their minds?

The brain tries to process complex movements and ideas under extreme stress. During elevated stress, there is an uneasy connection between its two main areas, the prefrontal cortex and the limbic system.

The prefrontal cortex, which is the most evolved brain region after the age of twenty-five, serves our highest-order cognitive abilities (like decision making). But it is the most sensitive to the detrimental effects of stress exposure. Uncontrollable stress can cause a rapid and dramatic loss of prefrontal cognitive abilities, which also include differentiating among conflicting thoughts, determining good from bad, future consequences of current activities, and social "control" (the ability to suppress urges that, if not suppressed, could lead to socially unacceptable outcomes).

Was there any foresight into the choices made on that twenty-minute hike up to Nick's grave? Or did the cognitive abilities of these twenty-year-olds completely shut down? Were they simply unable to identify the future consequences of their current activities?

The second part of the brain that is affected during elevated bouts of stress is the limbic system. The limbic system has an ultrapowerful reaction to our sense of being threatened. If we feel we're in danger, the limbic system puts us on high alert. Our body physically prepares for fight or flight, and we instantaneously have an enormous amount of adrenaline to freeze, run away, or attack the danger head-on. This was what Nick was experiencing but couldn't act on—his hands were bound behind his back and his mouth and part of his nose were duct-taped.

Whether it was done to provide a false sense of security or not, Rugge told Nick he wasn't going to hurt him. Hoyt wouldn't make that claim.

> Where is the boy
> Who looks after the sheep?
> He's under a haystack,
> Fast asleep.

Hoyt struck Nick in the head with a shovel. Nick dropped to his knees. And twenty-five minutes after they ascended to Lizard's Mouth rock, Hoyt squeezed the trigger on that TEC-9. Nine bullets riddled Nick from the waist all the way to his head. It would have been more if the gun hadn't jammed.

Rugge vomited. Hoyt then tucked the gun under Nick's leg

and proceeded to do a haphazard job of burying the innocent teen.

After another twenty-five to thirty minutes, Rugge and Hoyt returned to the car. Hoyt reflected, "That's the first time I ever did anybody. I didn't know he would go that quick."

And Little Boy Blue? Still wearing his father's ring.

It wouldn't matter that Jack Hollywood would hear about his son from Hogg, prompting the return drive home from up north. It wouldn't matter that Jack and his son briefly spoke on a pay phone, or that he would arrive at one a.m. that night, on August 9, to meet his son at Lasher's home. It wouldn't matter that Hollywood was, according to Jack, "kind of evasive" and "seemed very scared and confused." Or how Hollywood would tell his father that "some of his friends were holding a kid . . . and that they were worried that they were in some kind of trouble."

It wouldn't matter that when Jack pressed for more details, Hollywood tried to defuse the situation, telling his father that "the kid was just up there having ribs and drinking beers with some friends of his," but never said with whom.

It didn't matter that still no one contacted the authorities.

What did matter was how Hollywood failed to disclose the most important details. How he had earlier spoken around eight thirty p.m. to Rugge to find out the location of the Lemon Tree where Nick was indulging in more than just beer, being plied with Valium, weed, and Jack Daniels. How he was being narcotized in order for him to be as oblivious as possible to Hollywood's plan and its outcome at Lizard's Mouth. It didn't matter what Jack Hollywood would find out about the kidnapped boy. Because up at Lizard's Mouth? The murder was complete. Only Jesse Hollywood knew the details.

The Indian American philanthropist Manoj Bhargava has stated, "There's an old story about a blind man heading towards a well, and there's a guy who's watching. If the blind man falls into the well, who gets the blame? If you're watching something you can prevent, you've got to do something."

How many witnesses stated, *I don't want to get involved*, or *I thought it would just blow over*? What of the parents or enablers or an affluent culture that might have provided that false sense of being untouchable? There might have been a single grave that night, but there were countless "wells" along the way. When it came to the witnesses, where was their Kirk Miyashiro? Someone to provide the guidance to do the right thing?

Chapter 17

ESCAPE PLANS

ON AUGUST 9, THE DAY OF THE MURDER, HOLLY-wood acted quickly to collect money people owed him. He contacted Brian Affronti—Skidmore's friend who pretended he had a date when the van with Nick had reached Santa Barbara. Affronti's debt was four thousand dollars. Because he was at work, Affronti told him "to go to my house and pick it up." The majority was for a marijuana debt and money he had borrowed.

Hollywood had previously left a shotgun wrapped in a sleeping bag at Affronti's because he didn't want to drive around with it. Affronti told him to grab the sleeping bag along with the money. "That way it wouldn't look odd to my parents."

Hollywood also sold his Mercedes and bought a 2000 Lincoln LS. He withdrew twenty-five thousand dollars from a money market account. Hollywood was already thinking ahead, planning his getaway.

Ryan Hoyt suddenly had money. The guy who *owed* money now had it to burn. Hollywood, Hoyt, Skidmore, and Sheehan were all hanging in a parking lot. Everyone knew what had happened at Lizard's Mouth, or at least suspected what had happened. But no one spoke up about it. It was a sore subject. What wasn't a sore subject was how Hoyt promptly went to a surf shop and bought new clothes.

Graham Pressley told Natasha Adams that same day that he personally had driven Nick and Jesse Rugge back to Los Angeles. Natasha was relieved to hear Nick was home. Pressley fed her the story that "Hollywood came to the hotel and laid a gun on the bed, a TEC-9," to scare Nick, to "make sure that he wouldn't say anything." When she pushed to find out where exactly Pressley had dropped off Nick, all he could respond was, "I just dropped him off." He was acting strange.

Rugge called her later in the day just to say hi and tell her that he was staying at his mom's house for a week. He was "really happy and joking around."

Natasha, who had previously consulted with her mother about Nick being kidnapped, was relieved to inform her mother that Nick "had been taken home and everything was fine." In five days, that would all change.

* * *

A day after Nick's murder, Casey Sheehan hosted a cocaine-fueled party for Hoyt's twenty-first birthday. Hoyt did more than just celebrate turning a year older. He celebrated how he had committed his first homicide.

William Skidmore was one of the partygoers in whom Hoyt confided. Skidmore said Hoyt told him he'd hit Nick over the head with the corner of the shovel, the sharp part. Nick fell down on his knees and then Hoyt shot him. Skidmore said Hoyt wasn't expecting such powerful recoil, so when he pulled the trigger, he told Skidmore, "the gun just went up." It *walked itself* up Nick. He told Skidmore the bullets hit off the corner of Nick's head. According to Skidmore, Hoyt "kept bragging about that." Hoyt even added weapon onomatopoeia, imitating the sound of the TEC-9 as it fired, "Yeah, man, I did this [shooting], *b-r-r-r-r-r-r-r-r-r-r-r.*"

Hoyt also told Skidmore that Jesse Hollywood wanted Nick killed because what if he ended up going to the police once released? Hollywood had told Hoyt to find a place to hide him.

When Hoyt mentioned that he had used the "little gun," Skidmore knew that meant the TEC-9.

Skidmore was in shock. He couldn't believe Hoyt had killed Nick. Skidmore hadn't had any contact with the crew since he'd left Hoeflinger's place the previous weekend. Skidmore thought "it was pretty sick." He was trying to comprehend the enormity of the situation and couldn't. He just couldn't believe Hoyt kept bragging about it. He didn't think Ryan was "that callous." He knew Hoyt had problems at home and was "always whining about his stepmom," but if he had to picture this scenario . . . if someone asked him if he could see Hoyt pulling the trigger? *No. Never.* So then why did he do it? Skidmore knew only one reason—it was a way for Hoyt to clear his debt.

Hollywood drove three hours with his mother to Palm Springs to visit his girlfriend at a modeling convention. This might be the last time he saw her for a long time.

Jack Hollywood would also meet his son in Palm Springs. Jack said he was simply there to meet his wife, stay overnight, then drive home with her. Even though Hollywood was conveniently nearby, Jack said he never saw his son.

Chapter 18

A GRUESOME DISCOVERY

ON AUGUST 12, TODD FONTAINE, A SUPERVISOR FOR a construction company, took his first hiking trip to Lizard's Mouth with his wife and her friend. At around one p.m., they took a narrow trail so that when they entered it, they were "committed to following" it through. There they were met with a smell that was very pungent, and "loud." That was the only way Fontaine could describe it. The closer they approached, the more they saw flies hovering in the area.

Out of curiosity, they wanted to see what was causing the swarm. Fontaine picked up a branch and moved it aside. "The flies were even more intense underneath the branch." Fontaine's wife stepped beside him and "used her foot and kicked the dirt aside." At that point they saw "a pair of pants and a bloodstain." It took a second to process, but after seeing a left front leg from the hip to the knee and the zipper, Fontaine knew it was a "dead person, buried."

* * *

An hour later, Dr. George Sterbenz, a forensic pathologist, showed up at the scene. The temperature was over a hundred degrees. There were maggots and larvae covering Nick's eyes, nose, mouth, and, according to the pathologist, "the site of his injuries." It was impossible to visually identify him. Only his abdomen was protruding through the ground. Nick's hands were bound behind his back. Duct tape was covering his mouth and a part of his nose.

But inspecting the changes due to decomposition wasn't the only reason Dr. Sterbenz was summoned. He was also tasked with performing the autopsy.

Once Nick's body arrived at the morgue at Cottage Hospital in Santa Barbara, Dr. Sterbenz determined Nick had been shot nine times.

One lethal gunshot entered his jaw and exited the base of the skull. It traveled directly through his brain. There were other gunshots to his body that broke a rib or passed under his clavicle; seven that were considered "through-and-through," meaning they had cleanly entered and exited the body, but that single shot alone to the head was enough to end his life.

It took two days, but Nick was finally ID'd by fingerprints the police had on file for his sole arrest for marijuana possession. They also had a second point of reference to identify Nick—he was wearing his father's ring.

Susan Markowitz knew the second she heard the knock on the door. *Nick was dead.* It was just after six a.m. when detectives informed her of the details. At that point she went in and out of comprehending the situation. She caught fragments like "bullet riddled," and how her son's hands were bound behind his back.

When she was supposed to be coordinating his sixteenth birthday just over a month away, now she had to do the unthinkable: coordinate her son's six pallbearers. Carey Evans, now seventeen and one of Nick's close friends, would be one of them.

Chapter 19

BREAKING NEWS

FIVE DAYS AFTER NICK'S MURDER, NATASHA'S MOTHER showed her an article in the *Santa Barbara News-Press*. Natasha's worst nightmare was confirmed. It was a picture of Nick next to an article about a murder. There had been an article the day before that mentioned that a body had been found at Lizard's Mouth but had yet to be identified. The article her mother showed her left no doubt. This was Nick Markowitz. Natasha started crying right away. She kept asking, "How could it happen?" She told her mother she had to talk to Graham Pressley and Jesse Rugge. Her mother told her she was going to set up an appointment with a lawyer for later in the day because she wanted her daughter to be granted immunity from prosecution once she came forth with the names of those involved.

After she took her parents to work, Natasha called Kelly Carpenter to tell her Nick was dead. She told her to come over.

With Kelly present and crying, Natasha called Rugge next. She had woken him up. She wanted to know one thing: *Had he seen the paper?* He had not. She started yelling at him over the phone. "You should look at it." He asked her why. She told him again, "Just go look at it." He couldn't find the paper, so she told him herself, "Nick's dead." Rugge's voice grew panicky. He told her, "It's not what you think." He asked her to come over so they could talk about it. She was angry and no longer wanted to speak to him, so she hung up.

Natasha then called Graham Pressley. She told him to read the paper. He didn't have one, so he told her he would look for one, then call her back. She wouldn't break the news.

Next, Natasha and Kelly headed to Rugge's. She handed the paper to him. They went to his room. He told them he wasn't involved and that he would never hurt Nick. They were beyond upset. They asked about his involvement. He told them, "I didn't do anything. I didn't do anything. I just handed him off to someone else."

Natasha tried to press for more details. Rugge would only say, "I didn't do it, I didn't do it." He told them they couldn't tell anyone or he would go to jail. He wanted to try and contact Hollywood. Rugge was nervous. He wasn't wearing a shirt, and according to Natasha, she could see his heart beating through his chest. He was trying not to cry. Then Pressley called Rugge. Pressley told Natasha to come over after she left Rugge's.

Pressley couldn't find a paper, so Natasha broke the news about Nick's death to him. According to Natasha, Pressley was "completely jaded, numb," and responded with only one word, "Oh." He wanted to know what Rugge had told her. "Nothing," she said. Pressley stuck with his story that he had driven Nick and Rugge to Los Angeles.

Nick's dean of students, Kirk Miyashiro, had a visceral reaction to the news. He was having coffee with his wife, Joni, reading about a kidnapping in the local paper. He didn't know Nick had gone missing. "It was a *total* surprise." He saw a picture of Nick and screamed at Joni, "This is my kid! This is Nick!" Kirk was in shock. He had *just* seen him, before the summer. Nick had been invited back to school. He had done "exactly what I wanted him to do."

Later that day, Natasha went to her mother's law office to meet with a lawyer named Dan Murphy. She told Murphy she knew "something about the death of this kid who has been found up in the Santa Barbara Mountains." Murphy got on the phone with some "court people" and got Natasha immunity. That meant she could not be prosecuted for anything that had happened, including her involvement. Two detectives came to interview her. She later met with the sheriff's office in Goleta. She gave them names. Arrests were soon to follow. Nathasha made the right choice in disclosing what information she knew. However, it was the timing of it that proved costly.

Chapter 20

THE ROUNDUP

JACK HOLLYWOOD AND HIS WIFE DROVE TOGETHER back to Los Angeles from Palm Springs. Jesse Hollywood and his girlfriend would drive back separately. Hollywood had already read news about Nick's body being discovered. He briefed Skidmore and told him to read up on it.

Once home, Hollywood and his girlfriend picked up Skidmore and drove to an exit off the 118 freeway. Since news had broken in the papers that Nick's body had been found, Hollywood pronounced, "I'm [a] ghost." He wanted to separate himself from all responsibility and get as far away from West Hills as possible.

Skidmore called Affronti to warn him not to say anything. Hollywood thought Affronti was a weak link, and Skidmore believed Hollywood would enact retribution if Affronti talked. Hollywood wanted Skidmore to give Affronti a beatdown. Skidmore refused. Skidmore wanted Affronti to know that if he saw Hollywood to be careful around him, because who knew what Hollywood might do? Affronti also read the article featuring the murder of a high school student. There was a school photo of the victim wearing a white tuxedo. If Affronti had doubts before, now there were none whatsoever. The picture was of Nick.

Hollywood and Michelle sped away to the Bellagio in Las Vegas. From there, they headed to Colorado Springs, where Hollywood had lived for four years as a teen.

On August 16 in Los Angeles, Jesse Rugge was tackled by police officers on his father's front lawn. Graham Pressley had peacefully surrendered himself to authorities. Ryan Hoyt would be arrested early the next morning at a pay phone down the street from Casey Sheehan's house. Sheehan was with Hoyt and would be temporarily taken into custody. Due to previous run-ins with the law and gang affiliations, William Skidmore's arrest drew the biggest coverage.

Skidmore was on the front porch when his mother was returning from McDonalds. He was on the cordless phone with his girlfriend. When he went to put a cigarette butt in the ashtray, he leaned over and heard a different voice talking on the phone: *"It's a positive identification."* And then, *"Suspect is on the front porch, we have a positive ID."* Skidmore didn't know it, but he was intercepting the police feed that mixed with his cordless.

He leaned back and couldn't hear it anymore. He told his girlfriend, "Hold on real quick, I need to do something." He ran inside the house and told her, "I'm going to call you right back." He hung up and then called her on another phone. Right when he did, the other line rang—it was the police and the hostage negotiation team.

The police had Skidmore lock up his mother's dog. His little nephew was on the couch watching TV. They told Skidmore to leave him and to walk out to the curb with his hands on his head. They were adamant in their command for him *not* to turn around.

As soon as he got to the curb, he looked to the side, and that was when cars pulled up. He started to hear helicopters.

He said he saw a couple of guys in army fatigues with sniper rifles. When they ran across the street, he quickly looked behind him and saw the guns pointing right at him. They told him, "Get down!" It was a frenetic scene. Other police officers were jumping over the wall that divided his house from his neighbor's. The arrest was being aired live. The broadcast showed that helicopters had been watching Skidmore's house for hours.

When Hollywood was two hundred miles out from Colorado, he called his father to let him know he had called an old friend. Hollywood then stopped calling his father. Jack Hollywood decided to call this friend's mother: "If he gets in contact with you . . . have him call me, we need to get him a lawyer, he needs to go and face this thing."

Jack Hollywood placed a second call. This time to an old friend, forty-seven-year-old football coach, Richard Dispenza, who was Jesse Hollywood's godfather. He wanted Dispenza to know that his son might be headed his way and to contact him immediately if he heard from his godson.

When they first arrived, Hollywood and his girlfriend—who was now being referred to as "Sue"—checked into a motel.

Later FBI followed leads to Dispenza's home in Colorado Springs where Dispenza told them Hollywood had stayed with him for a night. What he failed to disclose was that he had checked his godson into the local Ramada Inn for *three more nights*.

After catching wind of the investigators, Hollywood flew Lasher back to Los Angeles with his California driver license and a blue folder containing his business affairs. Hollywood then dumped two guns with the friend he told his father about during the drive out. He admitted he was on the run from the police. But his friend didn't want to become involved or contact authorities.

Three days later, on August 23, Dispenza told the FBI he had lied about knowing Hollywood's whereabouts. He said he thought his godson was headed back to California to turn himself in. Dispenza was arrested for "harboring a fugitive," then put on paid administrative leave from his high school.

Hollywood would then move on to the next person he felt might be able to provide a place to sleep—a friend from junior high, Chas Saulsbury, whom he had not seen since 1995.

Chapter 21

BURIAL

ON AUGUST 19, NICK MARKOWITZ WAS LAID TO REST AT Eden Memorial Park in Mission Hills on a sun-glazed hillside. More than three hundred mourners attended. Close to half were teenagers.

It would upset Carey Evans that people who he thought didn't know Nick would talk about him publicly as if they had been close. Carey felt they were trying to be part of his life after the fact, and be "part of the attention that the end of his life received." Carey soon realized that "people experience tragedy in their own ways, and one doesn't need to be particularly close to the center of a tragedy to be affected by it. Everyone in the West Valley experienced Nick's death regardless of whether they knew him." While some had lost a friend, son, or cousin, West Valley had "lost a sense of security."

At home, the only small comfort Susan Markowitz could

find was a praying mantis. *This was Nick,* she told herself.

But today at the funeral, there was another source of comfort. Susan was so numb, her mother-in-law had to tell her, "Look. Look up." As their limo drove onto the grounds, she saw what her mother-in-law was referring to: how many people were there for Nick. There was standing room only outside. They could not fit all the attendees inside.

Rabbi James Lee Kaufman, who presided, would comment, "There are deaths, such as this, when we can't shake an angry finger at God and say, 'Why?' We can only look to ourselves." All these witnesses, and not one stepped forward. In Latin it's *Qui tacet consentire videtur*—to be silent is to consent."

Carey Evans echoed this sentiment. "The pity of it all is how no one involved could seemingly stop a series of *escalatingly bad* decisions from ending up where it did." Lots of "complex things led those guys to kill Nick: stupidity, fear, cowardice, insecurity, arrogance, hubris, a need to belong. Not just malice."

For Carey, he realized at seventeen "that it was possible to die for stupid reasons and because of bad decisions" made by others or yourself. One thing Carey knew for certain was that anyone involved—on either side—would carry Nick's death with them for the rest of their lives. "The consequence of it is inescapable."

Chapter 22

AN OLD FRIEND

CHAS SAULSBURY AND JESSE HOLLYWOOD WOULD
spend the next six days together. In their first forty-eight hours,
Hollywood lied and said he had been "pickpocketed." He then
started telling more of the truth in increments. Hollywood's
narrative—according to Saulsbury—was that "his friends
had pretty much killed somebody." Hollywood would try and
extricate himself, saying he was "implicated but not involved."
Though Saulsbury hadn't seen his friend since '95, he had kept
tabs on Hollywood's reputation as "one of the larger suppliers
of marijuana in LA." Maybe this had something to do with the
murder?

No matter how nuanced the story that Hollywood presented
was, Saulsbury never misinterpreted one absolute—his old
friend was on the run. However, Hollywood had no issue with
being forthcoming about the sad fact that he'd had to dump that

brand-new Lincoln—the one he had been bragging about—at his godfather's house.

Saulsbury was reluctant, but ended up agreeing to drive Hollywood back to California for three thousand dollars. Saulsbury quickly threw together a bag, fed his "pet scorpions" some crickets, and began the twelve-hour drive from Colorado Springs to Las Vegas in his 1990 Audi. Hollywood didn't have any luggage besides a large Ziploc of hundred-dollar bills. They would stay in Las Vegas for a night.

Saulsbury began having second thoughts and tried to formulate a way to separate himself from the fugitive. But Hollywood was a good friend—"I didn't want to ditch him on the side of the road."

Saulsbury learned very early that Hollywood wouldn't be turning himself in for murder anytime soon. According to Saulsbury, Hollywood "didn't want to face it." He also learned that while driving with Nick, Hollywood not only had an AR-15 in the van, but also that TEC-9, "a big shotgun," and "some handguns."

Back in Los Angeles, Hollywood tried to massage the narrative. He didn't refer to Nick's abduction as a kidnapping. No, instead they'd "grabbed" Nick and taken him to Santa Barbara.

Hollywood relayed to Saulsbury his conversation with his lawyer. According to Saulsbury, Hollywood said Hogg advised him "he was in enough trouble already" and to "get rid of the kid."

Did Hollywood ever inform Saulsbury of his alleged conversation with Eddy Bachman, the other neighborhood drug dealer who knew Hollywood was going to kill Nick to make a point?

It seems the closest Hollywood would confess to orchestrating Nick's murder would be to call it a "group decision." Hollywood disclosed to Saulsbury that Hoyt was the shooter. Hollywood said Hoyt confirmed the murder and told him, "I took care of it." By this time Hollywood had made good on his promise to become a "ghost" and had left town.

Hollywood and Saulsbury stayed at the Country Inn in Calabasas, located in Los Angeles County. In their rented room, news of the murder was all over the television. At that point, Saulsbury turned off the television as Hollywood detailed the entire story in a half hour. As more specifics were being disclosed, the magnitude of his association with Hollywood struck a nerve. Saulsbury realized he had a made a "terrible decision."

Saulsbury now had a change of heart about being with Hollywood. He agreed to drop him off at John Roberts's house. Hollywood had expected Saulsbury to drive around the neighborhood and return in a few minutes. Saulsbury had other ideas. Hollywood went in and Saulsbury "pretty much took off." And for good reason. Saulsbury saw this "as the easiest opportunity to get away without too much drama." That was the last he heard from Hollywood.

Saulsbury drove back to Las Vegas, where he stayed in a prepaid room that they had booked for a couple of nights. Once back in Colorado Springs, he learned that the FBI had visited his workplace. He contacted his lawyer and turned himself in. After being granted immunity—in other words, he could not be prosecuted for his involvement with Hollywood in exchange for witness testimony—he was debriefed by a Colorado Springs detective and two LA County sheriffs.

Back in West Hills, Hollywood tried to obtain a fake ID from John Roberts. Roberts told him he couldn't do that. But he did send Hollywood off with ten grand. And like that, Hollywood went off the grid.

While Susan disappeared into her grief, Jesse Hollywood would also disappear and become the youngest person ever to appear on the FBI's Most Wanted list. However, behind the scenes, behind the news articles and relentless press on the Markowitzes' front lawn, there was one man relegated to the shadows of the case. He was thirty-six-year-old Santa Barbara Detective Mark Valencia. What Hollywood didn't know was that he wouldn't be the only person in this case to go off the grid. Valencia would disappear with him.

Chapter 23

THE HUNT IS ON

HOLLYWOOD HAD BEEN ELUDING INVESTIGATORS for close to four years when Valencia entered stage right.

His involvement with the case was so confidential, only a small pool of individuals within the department knew what he was tasked with doing. Initially, this small chain of command held meetings regarding how to approach going after the fugitive, what resources should be used and who should do it. Finally, Valencia was asked to be the guy. For two years, this was to be his sole assignment. "They turned me loose. It was actually unique as they allowed me to make decisions on the fly. They trusted me." He only turned to the chain of command when he needed funding. He updated them when necessary. "The less people that knew the better."

But to go off the map, Valencia could no longer identify as a "detective." To catch this fugitive, Valencia had to become a "regular civilian."

Valencia was an avid weight lifter and wore a sixteen-inch braided ponytail. He would cut his hair every three years and donate it to kids suffering from cancer. He had intense eyes and could make a point clearly without ever raising his voice.

Valencia was of local Native American descent—the Chumash—and had grown up on a reservation that instilled in him the ethos "Every elder's your uncle." His family could be traced back to this land *before it was Mexico*. Some of his ancestors fought in the Civil War. He would visit their gravestones, which read, FIRST NATIVE SCOUT PLATOON US CAVALRY.

Detective Valencia never knew his real last name. The Spanish converted his family name into a traditional Spanish one.

Even though he didn't know his real name, Valencia never had an identity crisis. He was used to different roles with different objectives. He enlisted in the Marines at seventeen, right out of high school, as part of the Rights of the Warrior and Rites of Passage, which provided young Native Americans this opportunity. He had to wait a year to officially join.

He served from 1987 to 1992, with stints in Tarawa and Okinawa, and two tours in the Gulf for Operations Desert Shield and Desert Storm. He then went back with the UN for the nuclear arms inspections. He was a helicopter air crewman, flying on CH-53 Echoes, a nephew to the Huey helicopter.

After the Marines, he knew he was a good fit for undercover work with the sheriff's department and the Department of Justice (DOJ). He thought he would fit right in working for a "paramilitary organization."

Valencia grew up rough, so he had an advantage over most people when it came to dealing with the street. He adapted to undercover work effortlessly. That included five years as a sniper for a SWAT team.

Under the DOJ he was a part of the task force SBRNET—Santa Barbara Regional Narcotics Enforcement Team. The task force was composed of a single officer from every law enforcement agency in Santa Barbara County. SBRNET took over when a dope case crossed from street level to major narcotics.

Valencia was first assigned to street gangs, then to major dope trafficking (DTOs, or drug trafficking organizations). He got selected to go to major crimes narcotics, which wasn't just garden-variety street crime—it was cartel-level investigations. That involved serious biker gangs who "didn't hide behind toy drives." After serving over five hundred warrants, he was called up for *this*.

This was the Jesse James Hollywood case, and he was officially tasked with finding the fugitive. Hollywood had been on the run for close to four years. This assignment, though, would require more than another identity change. This time, in order to do the job, Detective Valencia wasn't that former corporal in the Marine Corps or an undercover cop. He was no longer even Native American. He had to go above and beyond just changing his identity. He simply had to *cease to exist*.

The FBI, who is involved in any kidnapping case, learned about Hollywood's travels after the murder. Hollywood was seemingly everywhere and nowhere—Palm Springs with his girlfriend, Las Vegas at the Bellagio, Colorado Springs hiding out with Chas Saulsbury. But when Saulsbury left Hollywood at John Roberts's house and headed home to Colorado, Hollywood's trail went cold.

No one knew, but Hollywood had been spending a couple of weeks at a friend's trailer in the Mojave Desert. He drank a cold Coors Light and laughed when he watched the SWAT team tear gas John Roberts's home, thinking the fugitive was there.

Meanwhile, Susan teamed with her dear friend Randi. They'd met well before Nick was conceived. They'd both worked at a shop in Northridge, California, called the Hidden Cottage. Randi was the type of person you could call at two in the morning for any reason and she'd be available.

Randi had planned to take Susan on a getaway trip. It was the first year after Nick "had passed, or—he didn't pass, I hate using that word—the first year he was *taken*, she got me to go on a cruise. Half the trip I was in a fog." Susan appreciated the help she was getting, even though it wasn't through a doctor's office.

Susan had become addicted to anything and everything that could narcotize her pain. The cruise with Randi was even more therapeutic, because she was out in the world, away from the laborious hours spent passing out FBI's Most Wanted flyers and driving around in her car, which served as a moving billboard, advertising the case and contact information.

At El Camino Real High School, Susan would pass out key chains and flyers with additional contact information. But it was a testament to Susan's character that someone who was grieving for the loss of her son would also extend appreciation to and acknowledge those who stood by her side and Nick's. One person she specifically went to visit was Kirk Miyashiro.

It was only three weeks later that the fall term began. One of the first individuals through the school doors was Susan. She "came onto campus and brought Nick's yearbook." She went to Kirk's office and asked, "Kirk, do you mind signing Nick's yearbook?" Of course he'd sign it.

Kirk told Susan how horrified he felt. He repeated how Nick had been starting to find his way and had turned himself around. He couldn't comprehend the senselessness of it all. "And I just, I lost it."

Susan was very gracious. "She was thankful to me as far as taking Nick under my wing, giving him a chance." Kirk was "honored to sign his yearbook, that she would be thinking of me."

One statistic Kirk wasn't proud of was that during his eighteen years in the LA Unified School District—fifteen as a teacher, three as an administrator—he had lost eleven students. Most of them were killed at the hands of others. Nick was one of those eleven.

Being with Randi on their cruise had stoked the restlessness inside of Susan. Even each calming breath of ocean air couldn't quell the fiery resolve that fueled her quest to find Hollywood. She'd used the opportunity to hand out more flyers, pass out posters, and lead her own search party of two. She and Randi even flew to Canada. This didn't make Valencia happy. Someone in law enforcement had tipped her off that Hollywood was up north. But Valencia couldn't confront her yet because she had no idea he existed.

Susan admitted she was "messing up the FBI's investigation. "They had to come to me and say, 'Back off.'"

Valencia, who was working in tandem with the FBI, had to do the one thing that goes against every tenet in undercover work: he had to make himself *made*. In other words, out himself. "She didn't know I had been assigned to the case. I was doing extensive undercover work and had been for years. A lot of the work I did was underground, so when I was assigned to do this, we didn't tell anybody."

Valencia had already been up in Canada, following leads on Hollywood's whereabouts. Susan flew up there and found out that he might or might not be in that particular area. She started handing out more flyers. Valencia knew that was counterproductive. "Well, what does that do? It sends him back underground. Now I'm back to where I started."

Valencia wasn't indignant about this. There was nothing more he wanted than to catch Hollywood, so much so that he printed a picture of Nick off the Internet and carried it with him at all times.

Valencia "*did not* want to meet the family. It's not that I had anything against them, but there's a focus when it comes to chasing someone down—it's called a *rundown*. You never want to let your emotions affect any decisions you make. Meeting the family or knowing the victim would stimulate those emotions. You're now putting a person to a name. And then you meet the family, and you don't want to carry the burden of their grief and guilt on your shoulders while you're conducting investigations."

Valencia and his colleagues finally made the drive to Susan's. His intense eyes never tried to disguise the compassion and humanity behind them. He just knew that he never had any intention of Susan and Jeff knowing who he was at that time. But maybe his colleagues could reason with her? Maybe he wouldn't have to approach after all.

While his colleagues spoke to her and Jeff outside their home, Valencia decided to wait back in the car. "I don't know if they were buying it. They were impatient." This left Valencia no choice. "I got out of the car and introduced myself." When Susan saw that sixteen-inch braid and impressive musculature, it was the last person she was expecting. Susan felt they weren't doing their job. "She felt the lead was cold and no one was doing anything, which is why she stimulated press." Valencia didn't fault her. He understood that any parent who had lost a child might do the exact same thing.

Wanting your son's killer caught was one thing. Inserting yourself into the investigation? Valencia had to set the record straight, so he sat them down. He asked them point-blank, "Do you believe me when I tell you I'm working on this case?" He then proceeded to explain the way things were going to be. If they wanted him to do his job, they would have to "leave me alone and let me do it." He was direct and harsh about it, but being standoffish was what kept the emotion out of it. Susan and Jeff were such good people that even he had to ask himself, how do you not get attached?

There were a lot of things one might be able to mask, things he had been *trained* to mask. Whether it was an unconscious decision or on purpose, his rigid posture decompressed, his voice softened. The *father* in him surfaced. "I'm not a robot, but it was one of the buffers I had to put up." He had a fugitive to catch.

The FBI received a tip from Chicago. An agent phoned Valencia, told him they were doing surveillance on an apartment after grabbing a lead that Hollywood might be inside. A pizza deliveryman exited. They waited until he returned to the shop. That was when they grabbed him. They showed him a picture and asked, "Did this guy order?" And he ID'd who he thought was Hollywood. The agent asked Valencia one question. "We're sitting on the house right now. What do you want us to do?'"

If it really was Hollywood, Valencia told him that the UFAP arrest warrant—Unlawful Flight to Avoid Prosecution—was good. The problem was Valencia couldn't order them to search the apartment to find out if Hollywood was inside. "There's what's called a Steagald warrant here in California. If you're running from the law and you're hiding in your cousin's house, I don't have the right to invade your cousin's [property], waive his Fourth Amendment [which protects against unreasonable searches and seizures], to search for you. I have to write a paper to say why I know you're in this house, 'cause I'm going into someone else's house to search for you, so it was pretty much the same lines that we had to write another warrant. They had it locked down, but we couldn't search." Valencia caught the first plane to Chicago.

Finally, with the proper warrant, they entered the apartment. "There were maps of Brazil and Mexico and routes and there was just no one in there, nothing, maybe a floor mat. It was clearly a crash pad." Two things stood out. "There was a lot of money" and "a large amount of marijuana."

Another lead sent Valencia to a possible informant at the Cook County Jail in Chicago. He didn't know how this man was affiliated with the apartment, but when he interviewed him, Valencia found out he was from Southern California. He was tied into Hollywood's group. Valencia just didn't know his level of involvement. And he never would. The possible informant told Valencia, "Look, you're a nice guy, but I am more afraid of them"—meaning Hollywood and his father's connections—"than I am of you." According to Valencia, "He didn't say a word. He was in Cook County Jail and that thing's a dungeon. He'd rather do that than me getting him out to help with this case. He knew about the cops coming to the apartment." Valencia didn't "have a *twist* on him, so we moved on. He was just a kid, too, a peanut-head kid."

Chapter 24

A BREAK IN THE CASE

VALENCIA HAD BEEN ON THE CASE A LITTLE OVER eight months. Finally, while tracking Jack Hollywood's phone he learned that one of Hollywood's family members was headed to Brazil to visit Jesse. Through other intel, American investigators had suspected that Hollywood could have been in Brazil since 2002. "So it was Jack that we got up on. He was my primary target [for any leads] because following him? He actually *gave it up*"—intel on his son's whereabouts—"and didn't know it." Valencia knew one hard fact about Jack. "He set up his kid for failure from the word *go*."

In the beginning, Jack wasn't Valencia's primary focus. "He had come up in several major investigations. We have computer databases all over the United States." Jack's name was included. "If anybody sees him [in the database]," which included the FBI and that small chain of command within the department, they were advised to "contact me."

Just how was Valencia made aware of Jack's illicit behaviors? "The weirdest thing happened. An [undercover] crew from San Bernardino or Riverside, they're working a Colombian kilo-level case—coke, not weed." Valencia was working for the Department of Justice, so he didn't even know this crew. "The crooks show up in a car [to meet the undercover agents]—somebody wants twenty, thirty kilos, somebody has the money," but it turned out the suspect couldn't or wouldn't do the deal.

"The undercover agents and informants—it has nothing to do with my case—they put a tracker on his car. They're all Spanish speakers." By law the tracker could be placed on a car for only a month. Three weeks later, when law enforcement had no intention of following the vehicle except to stop it and covertly remove the tracker, Valencia received correspondence that "Jack was driving it." Valencia couldn't believe it. He had zero clue as to why Jack was there. Valencia only received the call because Jack had been "flagged" in the database.

Valencia used classified tracking techniques to keep up on Jack 24/7. "I knew where he was and what he was doing at all times. I would go in plainclothes and just watch him." Jack "gave it to us," the lead that would send Valencia to Brazil—after moving around seaside resort towns, Jesse Hollywood had planted himself for the last year in a small fishing village called Saquarema near Rio de Janeiro.

The FBI was in charge of the UFAP warrant. An agent by the name of Dave Cloney was assigned to it. He would head to Brazil with

Valencia. "Dave is one of my heroes, a very, *very* good guy. I have nothing but good things to say about that man—a true patriot."

Agent Cloney wasn't only a mentor; according to Valencia, "Guys like that make you a better cop." The state and the FBI didn't always see eye-to-eye. "I've had cases where I worked undercover and we were side by side and it didn't work out well just because of difference in legality. But as an agent? This guy—I haven't had a problem with any FBI agents, even the guys in Chicago."

Agent Cloney had taken over the Hollywood case on the FBI side from Agent Kevin Kelly, who was retiring. Cloney joined the case when it was four months old.

By continually tracking Jack's phone, Valencia learned that the distant family member visiting Rio de Janeiro would meet with Jesse Hollywood at an outdoor mall by the beach.

However, how could Valencia be sure that the tip he received about Hollywood being in Brazil would pan out? Hollywood had seemingly been spotted everywhere. Even Kirk Miyashiro had put his school on lockdown because reports had surfaced that Hollywood had been seen back in the area. Miyashiro was worried that Hollywood might have been looking for payback at the high school from which he'd previously been expelled

Valencia decided to trust his training and go back to square one. He pored over every interview police had conducted with Jack Hollywood. The sheriff's department had forgotten about "one of the original interviews dad had—it was on paper—it's in our police reports—dad had tried to make arrangements for him to go to Brazil, and people kind of forgot about that." When

Valencia went back and reread it, "I saw that he had contacted someone who was identified as getting his son to Brazil. That was week one of the murder. I wasn't involved in any of that."

Valencia also had another informant in Brazil. He tipped Valencia off that Jesse Hollywood was indeed there.

There was only one issue. Valencia couldn't travel to Brazil as a representative of law enforcement. He had zero legal authority, nor police powers in Brazil. The Brazilian Interpol was calling the shots. Valencia had to leave his shield behind and travel unarmed as a tourist, with nothing but his passport. He no longer existed in any police capacity. He was considered an advisor.

Jesse Hollywood had chosen Brazil for one reason alone. He had heard about an Englishman, Ronnie Biggs, who participated in the Great Train Robbery in the 1960s. Biggs fled to Brazil after learning that the country wouldn't extradite if that fugitive fathered a child by a local. Following in Biggs's footsteps, Hollywood linked up with Marcia Reis, who was ten years older. Reis was now six months pregnant with their first child. However, Hollywood wasn't aware that this specific law no longer existed. Now, because Hollywood was illegally residing in the country, Valencia didn't have to worry about the UFAP arrest warrant and had grounds for deportation.

Now twenty-five, Hollywood tried to keep a low profile in the fishing village, even though his photo did appear on a travel brochure. Locals knew him as the young gringo *Miguel*, or "Mike," who would jog the shore with his two pit bulls when he wasn't engaging in domestic or drunken arguments with his girlfriend and locals. In fact, he was known to start running his mouth as soon as he started drinking. Patrons would joke with him, calling him Mike Tyson. Hollywood would counter and tell them that while Tyson used his fists to defeat his opponents, "I use a base-ball bat to defeat mine."

Hollywood was living off twelve-hundred-dollar monthly checks sent by his family. The two-hundred-thousand-dollar home he used to hole up in was replaced by the shabby one-story abode, twenty paces from the beach.

While Hollywood was known to throw raging barbecues for out-of-town guests, Valencia was busy operating within a dif-ferent type of dynamics: working with Brazilian Interpol. "They were great. Their heart is in the game. They just didn't have the logistical equipment. We would do anything to help them out. They were very, *very* poor." Their police station was a 1920s naval building. The floor was almost dirt. "[They had] a hard, hard road ahead of them."

Valencia got on well with every member of Interpol. Except for one. And it was over a simple misunderstanding. The head of Interpol thought Valencia "was *the* sheriff of Santa Barbara County." As a courtesy, Valencia "brought all these pins [from the department] to hand out. I had run out by the time I had reached him, and I didn't know he was *the* boss of Interpol. And he was upset. In hierarchy, I should have given it to him first. I felt bad. He didn't understand I was just a ground troop. He thought I was his equal and didn't treat him as such." Valencia quickly reme-died the situation and placed a call for the department to send him more pins. The Brazilian agents thanked the "Big Indian," which was translated from Portuguese. They couldn't remember his name, so "Big Indian" was how they would refer to him. "I would hear that and would know they [were] talking about me. They were awesome. They were *in the cause*."

Valencia planned to be in Brazil for a week. Day six was when the arrest would go down. At one point, Valencia found himself at the iconic ninety-three-foot statue of Christ the Redeemer—Jesus, with outstretched arms. The cultural icon, composed of reinforced concrete, is perched atop Corcovado Mountain. It looms some 2,300 feet over Rio de Janeiro and Guanabara Bay. But Valencia wasn't up there to enjoy one of the Seven Wonders of the World. He had undercover work to perform on Jesse Hollywood—a type of surveillance that he would never be allowed to publicly disclose. This "tourist" decided that day to wear a seemingly innocuous tank top, showcasing sleeved-out tattoos from elbows to shoulders.

One particular tattoo on his shoulder that stuck out was a "red condor over a skull" with the image of the sun. Valencia, thirty-six, had it done in his twenties. It held reverential significance. (He had to wait to get all his tattoos because he had wanted to do recon in the Marine Corps—they discouraged identifying marks.)

Valencia took to heart an old legend. "The condor is one of our sacred birds, and there's a story where it got too arrogant and flew too close to the sun, which is why it's now black." The skull on his shoulder had a red condor on it to always remind him to remain grounded. "Know your capabilities, know your limitations." What the skull represented was simple. "What's the end result of arrogance? Of being too overzealous, forgetting your roots?" The condor was purposely inked in red and not black. Valencia knew you had to maintain honor "by staying *red*." By staying grounded. This same insight could have benefited Jesse James Hollywood.

However, locals regarded Valencia's tattoo as the mark of an assassin. A profession for which Valencia—after spending five years as a sniper on a SWAT team—definitely possessed the parallel skill set. He finished up the undercover work at Christ the Redeemer and left without incident or compromising the ticking clock on the investigation.

However, there was one small hiccup Valencia hoped would not compromise the arrest. Due to "an error" made "during calibration of the equipment," one of Valencia's colleagues accidentally phoned Hollywood on his cell phone. The problem was that the caller spoke English to him, not the country's official language, Portuguese. It took a moment to realize it was Hollywood who had been called. The colleague quickly hung up. Was the investigation now compromised? Would Hollywood grow suspicious and flee? No one knew. They would have to wait and see.

Valencia never touched alcohol. If he was ever going to have a drink to calm his nerves due to a mishap, he saw this as a good enough reason as any.

Chapter 25

GO TIME

THE ARREST WOULD HAPPEN ON DAY SIX. THERE
would be no day seven. No, that day was reserved for the sixteen-
hour flight stateside.

Interpol was informed of the logistics—Hollywood had
not seen this family member for some time and wasn't sure of
the woman he was looking for. He would know her when she
approached. Valencia made sure that meeting never happened.
He would send in an undercover agent in her place. The only
obstacle? He had to keep the real family member from showing
up. Through intel, he knew she would be riding on a commuter
bus, then meeting at a table at an outdoor mall. What were his
options? He couldn't detain her on some bogus charge—he
technically wasn't even law enforcement. He didn't want her
arrested alongside Hollywood. She could present unknown
variables. Valencia, Agent Cloney, and Interpol decided on the

path of least resistance instead. As Hollywood's family friend was en route, Valencia ordered the bus she was commuting on to be pulled over. The bogus reason? *Passenger count and weight inspection.* It was a surreal moment for Valencia as he proceeded to drive around the stationary bus en route to the meeting spot to arrest Hollywood. He had been given two years to find the fugitive. Now these last eight months on the case—and nearly five years after Nick's murder—would come down to these next fifteen minutes. That was all the time they could buy until the bus was back up and running. It turned out, that was all they would need.

Valencia was at the meeting spot. It was, in Valencia's words, "a violent scene" when they took Hollywood down. The undercover officer approached Hollywood and made the initial arrest. That set off a preconditioned response by terrified locals. "A lot of kidnapping goes on." This was the assumption. After all, every one of the officers were plainclothes. Marcia Reis began screaming, "Kidnap, kidnap!" Even the military police were convinced, drawing their "long guns."

The scene was chaotic and had reached a boiling point. "Other agencies rolled in and were pointing guns at everybody." Over shouted commands, Interpol finally reasoned with the military police. It was a standoff where Valencia was helpless to intervene. Observing, he couldn't even take part in the arrest. "I went over there as a 'vacation' on my Visa." So as a tourist, all he could do was *walk by*. His simple nod served to officially ID Hollywood as their guy. Thankfully, Hollywood hadn't gone as far as Ronnie Biggs and had plastic surgery.

But as surreal as the arrest turned out to be, the aftermath was just as bizarre. In fact, to Hollywood's girlfriend, it was as if it never happened, judging by her nonchalant attitude afterward. "When it was it all over," the mother of his child "got a Coke and walked away. It was like nothing."

One thing did put Valencia's mind at ease before the arrest. Hollywood's flip-flops. There would be no outrunning anyone. As soon as he saw what was on the fugitive's feet, Valencia knew, "It was over."

Michael Costa Giroux. That was what Hollywood's passport read. Valencia didn't know the alias, but the Brazilians did. Under duress from questioning, Hollywood remained defiant about his identity. "They were grilling him. He was a professional. I mean, he just knew the drill. His ID was in the name of a magistrate's son, and he had it set up pretty good that family names were all involved in government or corruption in Brazil." With bribes so prevalent in Brazil, Hollywood was hedging that he could use his politically affiliated name to buy off officials. "We didn't know that either. The Brazilians told us." Hollywood had also obtained a fake birth certificate at some point. "He got everything from his father. His dad loved his son, I give him that."

There was a ticking clock on transporting Hollywood back to the States. "When we arrested him, we were waiting for *the* next plane. We didn't want anything to go wrong." They had to buy tickets in a heartbeat. "There were a lot of issues behind what we did." Brazil "doesn't extradite for the death penalty." That was what Hollywood could possibly have been facing. "We circumvented that, but it was our job to get him home." He was deported for being in the country illegally.

During questioning, Valencia stayed in the shadows, blending into the background. Hollywood had no idea who he was or what department he represented. He thought Valencia was Interpol. "I just stood back, and you really don't know what nationality I was. In Brazil you can't tell about anybody. There's all nationalities, they all speak Portuguese."

But Valencia's patience had a sell-by date. "Somebody there spoke both Portuguese and English and was telling me what was going on. Finally I got tired of it. I introduced myself, told him who I was and where I was from, and you almost saw the life leave his body—*it was over.*"

Hollywood "fell back in his chair and reached out to shake" Valencia's hand. Hollywood was arrogant about the fact that he had been caught. So full of hubris he told the detective, "You're the one."

Interpol was stunned. "They were blown away because his Portuguese was almost perfect. They didn't believe me that we had the right guy. His ID, everything was perfect. *Perfect, perfect, perfect.*"

Valencia never once questioned the real identity of Michael Costa Giroux. "It's not like they have Live Scan, where I could scan his fingerprints and send them back home. There was just no way. And cell phones weren't working to take his picture. But I knew it was him. But the problem is, like, I'm five-eleven and healthy, and I had been chasing him for so long and staring at his pictures that I had imagined this big, menacing criminal. Then when I see him, he's just a little boy." Valencia couldn't believe it. "Just a little boy. That's all he was. That just made the wrong decision and wrong choices and has to live with them forever."

But wasn't Valencia worried about Hollywood making that first phone call home? And *buying* his way out of custody? After all, "Brazil is full of bribes." What Hollywood didn't know was that it was going to be impossible for the one man who might be able to manipulate his release—his father—to take action. Valencia had authored a warrant for Jack Hollywood that he timed to coincide with Hollywood's arrest. Hollywood "told detectives, 'I'm going to be released. I'm going to be released by morning. You don't know how it works down here.'"

Valencia wasn't intimidated or worried. He gave it right back to Hollywood: "I'll tell you what. If you *are* released by morning"— they were waiting for their flight—"I will shake your hand and say no hard feelings and be on my way. He didn't know I arrested dad already. Dad was in custody for another warrant, which we didn't even file. We just arrested dad to get him out of the picture in case phone calls were made. I just needed him on the plane and then he was mine. So we took dad out of the picture early."

And speaking of Jack Hollywood, Valencia had kept tabs on him before heading to Brazil. He didn't perform surveillance with binoculars from an unmarked vehicle three blocks away or from some second-story rooftop. No, Valencia was often *right next to him*. On the set of *Alpha Dog*, the 2007 movie that was loosely based on this case and featured Justin Timberlake, Jack Hollywood was hired as a consultant.

Valencia seamlessly blended in with the grips and the gaffers, carrying ropes and equipment. No one knew who he was, and for good reason. *He didn't exist.* On off days or downtime when the film wasn't shooting, Valencia would take surveillance to a new level. He would act as a random beachcomber on Jack Hollywood's trips to the ocean. "There was one time I was following his father." But Hollywood's father wasn't alone. One of the actors accompanied him. "They went to the beach and they were playing football like I would throw it to my son. It was really weird. He was interacting with this actor who was acting like his son. It was sad."

Jesse Hollywood didn't represent the ideals of what the Red Condor symbolized. But how could he? "His dad was a street-level doper, and that was the life he knew." Valencia knew Hollywood's origin as a dealer. "He started with Ecstasy, selling a couple tablets here and there, and his dad was teaching him how to switch up locations and do standard doper stuff."

Valencia couldn't believe a father would set up his son for such a downfall. "Jack [Hollywood] did create the situation. He doesn't understand it. He is essentially the snowflake in the avalanche."

Even though Jesse Hollywood was in custody, Valencia couldn't control his legal rights. After all, he was a tourist until Hollywood boarded the plane. He couldn't Mirandize him and record his statements. Any taped interview would have been inadmissible in court.

Valencia secured the last two first-class seats. His partner had to fly economy. Valencia made sure Hollywood wouldn't attract attention to himself or cause a scene on the plane. He instructed Hollywood on how he would behave prior to boarding. Because Valencia was no stranger to performing extraditions, he laid down his nonnegotiable ground rules. "There's a very standardized speech I have that if they disrupt the flight, they will hit the ground before the plane does. And I am very serious about that. But I have to be." What Hollywood didn't know? "We weren't armed." Valencia wasn't traveling with his issued .40 cal—only his stamped passport.

Hollywood had yet to be officially arrested. "As soon as he was deported, we just *happened to be there* to take custody of him, because you're in the custody of the country you're in transit to. Essentially, we arrested him on the plane."

That meant also binding him. "We had to buy handcuffs. We had to restrain him getting him on the plane. We had a hoodie, you put your hands in it." That was when Valencia cuffed him— with his wrists bound inside the sweatshirt's front pocket. None of the passengers had any clue.

Chapter 26

THE "RED CONDOR"

RETURNS

IT TOOK EIGHT MONTHS ON THE CASE, BUT IN MARCH 2005, Valencia finally escorted the fugitive home. As they spoke on the flight, Valencia arrived at one frightening conclusion about Hollywood. "He's a sociopath. He was going to survive any way he could. And it's too bad, he was just a kid. I wasn't worried. I wasn't afraid. And if you didn't know [who he was] and you were sitting in first class two seats down? It would have been just like two old chums yukking it up all the way back." But over the course of that sixteen-hour flight, when it was announced over the intercom how close they were to the States, Hollywood's demeanor slowly morphed. "I know that he loved his dad and that he feared his dad. And you can't change that in a person."

At the beginning of the flight, Hollywood was pretty much "tears and fear—and his whole worry, what was his dad going to think? What was his dad going to do? He got tougher because he had to put on a brave face."

When they finally landed, "reality was setting in." Hollywood "was actually somewhat relieved that it was over. I mean, imagine running at that age without a support system."

Hollywood remembered the cell phone call he'd inadvertently received from Valencia's colleague. He was kicking himself. It was in English. Even though that made his suspicion grow, he hadn't reacted. Now all he thought was, *how he should have gone on the run again.*

Valencia stopped the plane prior to taxiing. "It was a deportation, so we didn't want to release him to ICE [Immigration and Customs Enforcement]. He would have had the hearing and it would have been forever." With a warrant, they had to book him at the point of entry of Los Angeles. So on the tarmac, Valencia "dropped him out of the food door" and "had the state guys pick him up."

As for Valencia? "When we got out of the plane, all the cameras were there." Valencia could have turned opportunist, posing for pictures and interviews. After all, he had just apprehended the youngest fugitive ever to appear on the FBI's Most Wanted list. No, the Red Condor simply changed his shirt, got off with his luggage, and blended in. There was no hero's welcome. No town car waiting. In fact, Valencia didn't even have a ride home. "Nobody even knew." This was a man simply doing his job. The only thing left to do besides finding a ride home from the airport was to retire from his "special enforcement bureau," which also called for him to "relinquish the responsibilities" that came with it.

Valencia ended up gifting Hollywood's handcuffs to the retired Kevin Kelly, who'd been the FBI case agent before Dave Cloney.

Valencia hadn't slept in three days. Officially, he was done with the case. Unofficially, the case wasn't done with him.

Valencia knew he couldn't attend the trial. "I didn't exist. I was a tourist."

The district attorney's office "wanted to subpoena everything" that Hollywood had confessed to on the plane.

The original prosecuting attorney, Ron Zonen, had been taken off the case because he had spoken with the filmmakers on the movie. They didn't want any appearance of a conflict. Valencia had to now deal with Joshua Lynn, the district attorney assigned to prosecute Hollywood.

When Lynn approached Valencia for information, Valencia answered him with one word—*no*. "That was a big deal, because what he [Hollywood] talked about was as good as a statement can ever be, but I couldn't use it. He had given it up. They wanted to force me to say that." The DA then went after his sources. Valencia stated, "I will never turn in an informant, which is one of the reasons I was effective with informants. I'll throw a case before I give them up. All I had to do was bring him back. I don't care what you do with him after." Remember, *Detective* Valencia was never in Brazil.

Chapter 27

NINE YEARS

IN THE TIME BETWEEN NICK'S MURDER IN 2000 AND Hollywood's trial in 2009, the four other defendants had either had their trials and had been sentenced or had taken a plea deal.

Ryan Hoyt would be charged with first-degree murder and receive the death penalty. His trial began in October 2001 and ended in November of that year. He was convicted on November 20. He was sentenced to death on November 29, 2001. During his questioning with police, he downplayed his role in Nick's kidnapping and murder, stating, "All I did was kill him."

Jesse Rugge was charged with aiding in the kidnap and execution of Nick. He was convicted in 2002 and was sentenced to seven years to life in prison with the possibility of parole. After serving eleven years in state prison (and being incarcerated for a total of thirteen years), he was found suitable for parole.

During his police interrogation, he initially confessed to

duct-taping Nick's mouth and nose and helping with burying Nick. He could have possibly been charged with felony murder. The felony murder rule states that "any death which occurs during the commission of a felony is first-degree murder, and all participants in that felony or attempted felony can be charged with and found guilty of murder." If Rugge was found guilty, this could have potentially carried a conviction of life without the possibility of parole.

However, Rugge's police interview was ruled inadmissible in court due to police coercion. Rugge was threatened with getting the "needle"—the death penalty—if he didn't come clean. During his trial, Rugge testified that he decided to go his own way once the group reached Lizard's Mouth, stating he had no idea a murder was going to take place.

William Skidmore was charged with kidnapping and strong-armed robbery. He took a deal for nine years in September 2002 (including two years of time served after his arrest in 2000). He was released in April 2009. The print of his left ring finger was also found on a roll of duct tape on top of Richard Hoeflinger's nightstand in his bedroom. That placed him at the scene where he last saw Nick.

Graham Pressley was charged twice. In July 2002 he was acquitted of kidnapping. The jury was hung on the murder charge. In November 2002 he was convicted of second-degree murder. Because he was only seventeen at the time of the crime, he was incarcerated at a California Youth Authority facility until he turned twenty-five years of age in 2007.

When discussing those involved in Nick's murder, Detective Valencia drew a comparison from his extensive knowledge with members of the Mexican Mafia and motorcycle gangs. "Those guys are hardened criminals. They grew up in a lifestyle where their dad was a Hell's Angel or a Vago. Their whole life has been inundated with this lifestyle. Their life expectancy is only forty, because they chose that." But Hollywood and his crew? "I refer to them as MTV gangsters; they weren't impressive. They were wannabes. They weren't hard. I had dealt with some *real* bad dudes and they *earn* every bit of it."

Valencia's personal views didn't necessarily represent his department's. But what they both probably agreed on? He doesn't know what Hollywood and his crew were thinking and still couldn't even "digest what happened to this day." Valencia was certain of one thing: they flew too close to the sun. Unlike the sacred bird tattooed on his shoulder.

Chapter 28

FINALLY HERE

3242 . . . THAT WAS THE NUMBER OF DAYS SUSAN AND Jeff Markowitz had been waiting for Jesse Hollywood to testify. The day was Tuesday, June 23, 2009. Nearly nine years had passed.

In the time between Nick's murder and Hollywood's first day of testifying in Department 14, with Judge Brian Hill presiding, Susan Markowitz would escape to alcohol, prescription pills, and multiple suicide attempts. She would also spend countless nights sleeping in her only son's bed.

Santa Barbara's Spanish Colonial Revival courthouse was a historic site. But what it possessed in aesthetics, it lacked in functionality. It did not have an official "holding tank" to house Hollywood. No one wanted to risk escorting Hollywood through the main hall into the courtroom past media and the gallery. It was decided this hearing would be moved across the street to a quaint, nondescript building that didn't come with an elderly docent at the front entrance volunteering her time to set up free tours or answer questions about the historic site.

The trial had officially begun five weeks earlier, on May 15. District Attorney Joshua Lynn gave his opening statement to the jury: "Jesse James Hollywood murdered fifteen-year-old Nicholas Markowitz like he pulled the trigger himself."

He stated that while Nick was "being gagged and tied and beaten over the head with a shovel . . . and then right after he was shot dead," Jesse Hollywood was having dinner at the Outback Steakhouse. He declared that although the defendant had twenty-five thousand dollars on him, he instead paid with a credit card. The inference was that Hollywood was establishing an alibi.

As far as Ben's debt, not even another check cut by Jeff Markowitz would settle it. But why not? Ben's father had already paid off an earlier three-hundred-dollar debt, according to Lynn. So why wouldn't Hollywood accept another check? Even though he never spoke to Eddy Bachman, Lynn would cite the same motive for the killing as Bachman. In regard to Ben's drug debt and the consequences for it, "Hollywood felt disrespected." You couldn't put a price on your reputation. Lynn stated that Jesse Rugge was "trying in vain to get ahold of Jesse Hollywood. 'What's going on? Why do I still have this child at my house? What am I supposed to do with him?'"

Lynn would describe how despite having access to two of his girlfriend's cars, a BMW and a Jeep Cherokee, Hollywood would instead ask his friend Casey Sheehan to borrow his "thrashed, faded red Honda Civic." Hollywood left Sheehan's house, picked up Hoyt back at his house on Cohasset Street, then had Hoyt drop him back off at Sheehan's. "And nobody asks any questions." Hoyt used the Honda to head to the Lemon Tree with Hollywood's TEC-9.

After the murder, on August 10, Lynn described how Hollywood "goes to Van Nuys Motor Sales. He sells the Mercedes and rims. He's cashing out, ladies and gentlemen. He's leaving town. He's leaving everybody else to deal with the situation. And everything he does is about planning his escape."

At one point, Hollywood was no longer looking to collect Ben's debt. According to Lynn, he was instead placing a bounty on Ben. While describing Ryan Hoyt's birthday party over at Sheehan's house, Lynn stated, "A man named Scott Dumas walks over to Casey Sheehan and tells Casey Sheehan something that causes Casey to walk over and ask Jesse James Hollywood point-blank why he was offering money still at this point in time to harm Ben Markowitz." Lynn reminded the jury that Nick was dead at this point and had not yet been discovered, yet Hollywood was refocusing on the original target of his anger.

Lynn would close his opening statement by comparing Hollywood to an offensive coordinator in the NFL. "He's up in the box, way off the field, on the telephone barking orders, 'Call this play, call that play.'" To Lynn, he was a "ruthless coward."

Hollywood had two defense attorneys, Alex Kessel and James Blatt. Blatt would also give an opening statement on May 15.

He would paint Ben Markowitz as "the moving force of this accident." He told the jury that despite Ben's Jewish descent, "he has swastikas and other Nazi paraphernalia attached to his body." He added that Ben "had the nickname of Bugsy after the famous Jewish gangster, Bugsy Siegel."

Blatt would try and sell the jury on his client's narrative that Nick's kidnapping had ended once they arrived in Santa Barbara; that Nick was free to leave at any time. He would never refer to Nick "being kidnapped," but rather as being "taken."

Yet Blatt would leave out that no one, not even Hollywood, ever attempted to return Nick to his home. He would leave out the fact that Nick had told Kelly Carpenter and Natasha Adams that he didn't want to make any extra trouble for his brother, Ben.

Blatt tried to utilize sympathy to sway the jury. He mentioned Jesse's parents going through a divorce since Nick's murder, and how Jesse's younger brother suffered "from a congenital heart disease and had a bad heart from day one." Blatt tried to lessen the severity of Hollywood's role as a marijuana supplier, stating, "He was not this major player that controlled three million potential customers in the San Fernando Valley." Blatt wielded Michelle Lasher's Judaism to show that his "Christian" client was accepting of other beliefs and open-minded. He lastly accused Ben Markowitz of killing one of Hollywood's dogs. He would leave out the fact that Hollywood had an arsenal of firearms, from that AR-15 to handguns, to a shotgun, to the AK-40 he slept with on his nightstand. He would bring up the TEC-9, but not in terms of his client's ownership. No, he would lay the blame on someone else: Ryan Hoyt.

Blatt labeled Hoyt "a flake." Someone who "desired recognition," to the point that he would lie about joining the Navy SEALs and being a male model for Versace.

As far as Nick, Blatt stated to the jury that once he was in Santa Barbara, "he's talking to Mr. Hollywood on the couch and they're having a pleasant conversation."

After Nick's murder, he would say his client was livid with Ryan Hoyt, yelling, "How could you do that? You're f-ing crazy. Are you out of your mind?" His strategy was to redirect the interpretation of those questions as the summation, *How could you kill this kid?* from the actual meaning: *How could you leave the TEC-9 behind at the crime scene?* He would tell the jury that Hollywood even blew a blood vessel in his eye. And lastly, he would tell the jury the reason Hollywood took flight as a fugitive. He even tried to personalize it, "Would many of you or your sons or daughters have run if they're [the district attorney's office] looking for the death penalty?" He never brought up the point that if his client was innocent, whatever the district attorney sought would have been an arbitrary point.

He ended his opening statement with a comment aimed at District Attorney Lynn in regard to proving Hollywood's guilt. "Johnny Unitas had one saying before the first play in the huddle of every game. . . . 'Talk is cheap, now let him prove it.'"

Five weeks and some two dozen witnesses later, Day 3242 finally arrived. It began promptly at nine thirty a.m. The defense's first witness—Jesse James Hollywood.

*　*　*

Susan Markowitz had a volatile reaction when she first laid eyes on the defendant. Finally, after all these years. Here he was. For the world to see. She heard he had actually been to her house at some point. She didn't remember. Now all she could think was, "What a *frickin' measly coward* to have to hire people to try and save you? From what?"

She also noticed how profusely the defendant was perspiring. "His palms were sweating, his face was sweating as if we were in a steam box. And he kept drinking Smartwater. And I kept thinking to myself, it's a little late to be drinking *Smart*water."

Under direct examination from his attorney, James Blatt, Hollywood answered that he had lived in Colorado between the ages of thirteen and sixteen. This was when he began selling small quantities of weed.

His father owned a sports bar at the time, along with operating his own marijuana business. Hollywood testified, "I always had an idea that my father was in illicit activity, but my father was always professional and never—he was never the type of guy to do anything, any type of transactions or anything illegal in front of his family, nothing that I ever saw when I was a kid."

When his family returned to Los Angeles, Hollywood stated, back and shoulder problems ended a promising baseball career. His pitching days over, he dove straight into the dope game.

Michelle Lasher had been his high school sweetheart. "She sat in front of me . . . and we were inseparable after that." She would eventually have *Jesse James*, eight inches long and two inches high, tattooed on the small of her back.

Hollywood would tell the jury that his father was involved in "low- to mid-grade marijuana in very high volumes." His father's market was in New York, "bringing hundreds of pounds in California." Hollywood would talk about his own territory: "My market was more a market that I created in the Valley— mostly high-grade."

During the time he moved into his first home at eighteen, he was pulling in eight thousand dollars a month.

Blatt would change course and question Hollywood about Ryan Hoyt, asking Hollywood to describe his relationship with Hoyt. "His mom had mental problems, and his dad was very abusive and alcoholic."

Blatt would follow up with more questions about Hollywood's seemingly positive attributes. Hollywood would explain how he was always on a diet, "didn't party too frequently because I was . . . taking care of my business and my business was always first." He would proudly state how he started building up his credit at a young age. His FICO score was "seven fifty to seven eighty."

By the time he upgraded to his second home a year later, he was making ten thousand dollars a month.

He would state that he met Ben Markowitz through Ryan Hoyt, who brought him into the marijuana scene as a dealer on consignment.

During this period, Hoyt had accrued his own debt, "so we sanded the Jacuzzi down" and had Hoyt put in "new turf" in the backyard that had been destroyed by his dogs. He had Hoyt do any odd job to start chipping away at the money he owed.

Blatt didn't refer to Nick's abduction as a kidnapping, rather vaguely describing it as "this incident." At the time, Hollywood said Hoyt owed him only a hundred dollars, maybe to distance himself from a motive to have Hoyt pay off a higher debt by killing Nick.

On day two of his testimony, Blatt had Hollywood explain the relationship he had with Ben Markowitz. Ben had lived with Hollywood for a period of two to three months, paying two hundred dollars a month in rent. Jeff Markowitz wrote the check. Hollywood would describe how he accepted a TEC-9 in exchange for a five-hundred-dollar drug debt from another friend who sold for him on consignment. He said that Ben was the one who suggested having its trigger shaved.

Blatt never directly asked Hollywood the identity of his marijuana supplier. Instead he tried to distance Hollywood from that TEC-9, asking Hollywood what happened to the gun after they had visited a shooting range. Hollywood replied that after finding out the gun was illegal, he went to Ryan Hoyt's grandma's house and "left the gun there in his garage."

At this time, Ben had assumed possession of the "bunk" Ecstasy pills. Hollywood testified that he handed one to Michelle Lasher to test. "We gave her one of the pills to see if it was good and she said it was good." He would say Ben gave him "the whole story" that it was no good, then explained to the court, if "you had one hundred pills, and you give out ten of them and they're no good . . . you bring the guy the other ninety back and say, here,

here's your ninety pills, they're no good, you can find out for yourself. He did not do that." No, he stated that Ben had "taken the money for himself." Hollywood told the court Ben wanted more marijuana fronted to him, but Hollywood declined. Ben was said to owe him twenty-five hundred dollars.

Hollywood testified that he spread word around his dealing circles to write Ben off, that he wasn't good on his word to pay back any debt. He then told a very different tale about encountering Ben's fiancée at BJ's Restaurant and Brewhouse where she was a server.

Hollywood became angry when he saw the diamond ring she was wearing and found out that Ben had just gotten a new apartment. He told Ben's fiancée that Ben had been ducking him and owed him. "She seemed very embarrassed." He would also ask her, "Why are you with this guy?" Hollywood testified that she said Ben "does this to everybody." She then said, according to Hollywood, "You guys don't have to pay for this." He didn't pay the thirty-five-dollar tab, instead telling her, "Take fifty dollars off Ben's debt."

He told the jury, "I wasn't trying to do this maliciously or to provoke Ben, either." He told the court he regretted his actions. "That's kind of what set Ben off."

From there the threats started. According to Hollywood, Ben would leave messages on his voice mail like, "You better be packing," meaning he'd better have a gun. "I have two nines," meaning two nine-millimeter pistols. "I'm not the type of guy to talk things out."

After the restaurant incident, Hollywood claimed his dog was poisoned and died. He stated that two days later Ben had called up to say vindictively, "Sorry to hear about your dog."

Hollywood also stated that Ben left the veiled threat, "I know where your mom lives." He interpreted that as a threat against his entire family who lived at his mother's.

According to Hollywood, Ben summed himself up the best during his own testimony. "When Ben was up here, he described it best when he said he's a snake in the grass." After Ben told Casey Sheehan to relay the message to Hollywood, "Tell Jesse he better be packing, I'm packing," Hollywood stated he turned to John Roberts for firearms in the form of a pistol and an AR-15.

Hollywood said he went to his lawyer, Stephen Hogg, for advice. He told Hogg that Ben "was coming after me like *Cape Fear*," in reference to a movie in which Robert De Niro plays a jilted character out for revenge.

Blatt had Hollywood remind the court that he had been on the run for four and a half years and in custody the same amount of time. It had taken this long to bring him to trial due to preparations, which included interviewing witnesses and reviewing all case evidence on both sides.

Hollywood said that he regretted "being in that whole lifestyle." Blatt formed questions in order for his client to downplay his reputation as a drug kingpin. Hollywood didn't buy jewelry, take expensive vacations or purchase a lot of clothes. Similarly, Blatt would downplay Nick's kidnapping and murder by referring to it as "the incident with Mr. Nick Markowitz."

Hollywood testified about the day his windows were broken. He claimed Ben called up to ask, "How did you like that window job?" and then told him, "This is just the beginning, motherfucker."

When asked about the events of August 6, he stated, "I wanted to confront Ben and end this." He said it was futile to call Ben, yet told him to "come over right now and we'll settle this," in a one-on-one fight.

Hollywood stated he wasn't on his way to break windows at the Markowitz home when he, Jesse Rugge, and William Skidmore piled into that white van. No, he said they were driving to pick up Brian Affronti, en route to Fiesta in Santa Barbara. That was when he spotted Nick walking down the street. "I got out of the van and I pinned him up against a tree and I said, 'Where's your brother?'" He said Skidmore punched Nick in the stomach and then "ushered" him into the van.

He would testify that everything happened very quickly. That Skidmore checked Nick's pockets and took weed, Valium, and his wallet. Hollywood would tactically leave out the fact that he commandeered Nick's pager. He didn't recall Nick's ring.

When asked why he didn't just let Nick go once Nick said he didn't know where Ben was, Hollywood could only respond, "I should have. I don't know why I didn't."

On the drive to Santa Barbara, Hollywood testified, Nick said Ben "was always a problem."

Blatt would downplay the kidnapping once again by referring to it as "the taking of Nick Markowitz." Hollywood made no attempts to call Ben or the Markowitz family.

Hollywood would state that Nick was intimidated after being pinned against the tree and punched in the stomach. He said Nick "had a scrape on his elbow."

Once in Santa Barbara, Hollywood claimed he tried to play peacemaker to the extent that even though he had borrowed a van, he was trying to get a ride home from another friend. "I felt—right when we arrived there with everything that was happening, I felt William Skidmore was being really aggressive and I wanted to de-escalate the situation." He said this was why he gave the keys to Skidmore and Affronti to head back to Los Angeles, not because they mentioned they had dates. But if he truly wanted to "de-escalate" the situation, *why not just have Skidmore drive Nick home?*

Hollywood told the jury he ordered Skidmore to untape Nick when they were at Richard Hoeflinger's apartment. In Hollywood's eyes, things might have appeared very casual. "We hand Nick the menu and he said what he wanted to eat." He said Nick was playing video games and "hanging out" like everybody else. Hollywood stated, "He was free to go. I mean, he was free to do whatever he was going to do in that house."

Blatt would again question Hollywood about his thoughts while Nick was at Hoeflinger's apartment. "I was kind of sidetracked." But not with the fact that he had committed a kidnapping. No, he would mention how he had wanted to go to Fiesta, how he was still upset over Ben breaking his windows, and lastly how he was going to be showing his house that week. Those were, according to his own testimony, his pressing concerns.

Skidmore and Affronti had left by this point but had returned because Affronti had forgotten his cell phone. When they returned, Hollywood "was on the couch, I believe with Nick, playing video games." Yet a second opportunity, and he didn't elect to send Nick back to the Valley.

A friend would eventually pick Hollywood up. For the third time that day, Hollywood could have "de-escalated the situation" by giving Nick a ride home. He did not. He left him in Santa Barbara with Jesse Rugge.

He kept repeating himself to the jury: "I had to show my house, I had these windows broken. I was sidetracked." He had a "million things," including his "business," that needed priority. Nick wasn't one of them.

Hollywood testified that when he finally returned to the Valley, he did make one phone call. But it wasn't to the Markowitz family or to his trusted attorney. It was to Mission Burrito, to order some food.

Hollywood stated that Jesse Rugge had told him to come up the following day, August 7, to collect five hundred dollars he was owed. He said that the abducted teen "was in no danger. Honestly, I wasn't really thinking about Nick Markowitz."

Hollywood said that he did go to Rugge's the next day with Michelle Lasher. He said he did see Nick when "I went upstairs to use the bathroom." He testified that they "smoked some pot in Rugge's bedroom." He says he specifically asked Nick, "Do you want to come back to the Valley with us?" Nick allegedly replied, "No, I'm cool."

Hollywood would go on to reiterate that he never thought Nick was in any danger.

On August 8, Hollywood said, he was back in the Valley because he had to meet with his cousin Jerry Hollywood, who was looking for condos for him.

Hollywood decided that day to also meet with Stephen Hogg because "I was concerned about the initial taking of Nick." He told Hogg that Nick had been taken from the Valley to Santa Barbara and "was released after that and free to go pretty much." He did what he could to, in his words, minimize his involvement.

Hollywood stated he wasn't concerned about Hogg mentioning a penalty for kidnapping for ransom. As Hollywood understood it, someone would have to call and demand money for the abductee's release.

Hollywood never went to the police, he stated, because of his "illicit activities." He didn't "want to get my friends in trouble." He testified that when he spoke to Rugge, Rugge had asked him to come pick him and Nick up and take him back to the Valley, where his mother lived. But Hollywood stated that he didn't have a car and Michelle Lasher's was a lease and couldn't spare the miles. When did he suddenly no longer have access to that white van? Instead, Hollywood sent Hoyt in Casey Sheehan's car to Santa Barbara to pick up them up. Hollywood then went with Casey Sheehan and Lasher to Outback Steakhouse to celebrate her birthday. This was the dinner he would pay for with his credit card.

Hollywood testified that he called his cousin Jerry Hollywood later that night at around ten thirty p.m. The conversation went from Hollywood asking if he had gotten his house listed, to whether his cousin had found him a new condo to move into, and then to Nick. Jerry Hollywood, now seventy years old, had testified earlier in the trial that Jesse told him "someone was taking the boy home." But his cousin's testimony cast a lot of doubt. Lynn told Judge Hill that he believed Hollywood's defense investigator had "helped" Jerry remember the phone conversation; Jerry Hollywood said the statements he made were accurate but that "they just weren't my own words."

Hollywood then stated that on August 9, he spoke to Hoyt, who said he'd taken Nick home. But on August 10, Hollywood had the infamous conversation at Hoyt's birthday party, held at Casey Sheehan's. Hollywood testified that Hoyt told him "he fucked up." Hoyt would admit to killing Nick. Hollywood said his response to that admittance was "What the fuck were you thinking?" Others testified that that was in reference to Hoyt leaving Hollywood's TEC-9 behind at the crime scene.

Hollywood would go to Palm Springs with his mother and pick up Michelle Lasher. He testified that he didn't go to the police because "it didn't fully dawn on me until it was on the news what had happened." Hollywood told the jury that when Skidmore broke the news that Nick's body had been found, he stated, "I'm [a] ghost," as slang for "I'm leaving this area."

Hollywood testified that he was afraid of how "our world had just become everyone's world." He had used this phrase once before. He was "shocked" that Hoyt "had actually done this."

Hollywood fled with Lasher to Las Vegas, where they got a room at the Bellagio for the night. He testified that it was "stupid" how he "just blew the money" on that expensive room. Hollywood beat himself up for paying for a pricey hotel, but not over the murder of a fifteen-year-old boy?

From there, he confirmed his transgressions in Colorado Springs and how he eventually linked up with Chas Saulsbury. He then testified that he paid Chas three thousand dollars to drive him back to Los Angeles.

He spoke of how they were "hotboxing in the car," which prolonged the trip home. As more time went on, Hollywood said he informed his friend of how the killing went down, but was adamant that "I was innocent." He went as far as to invoke divine guidance. "I was definitely praying, crossing myself and asking God to help me at that point in time." But help with what? To do the right thing or to not get caught?

Chas would drop him off at John Roberts's place. Roberts would send him off with ten thousand dollars. He was picked up by another friend, who let him stay in his trailer in the Mojave Desert for three weeks. It was in an area where "they wouldn't even deliver mail because it was such a dangerous place." As he tells it, he went to a supermarket and "got some beer and frozen food and cigarettes." Though he claimed he was innocent, he never tried to turn himself in to proclaim just that. No, he stated he was scared off by the show *America's Most Wanted*, which ran with the motive that Hollywood had kidnapped Ben Markowitz's brother over an unpaid drug debt.

He stated he "had no hope." That this was a "death penalty" case. That he "had already been convicted in the media." So then he obtained a fake ID from someplace in downtown Los Angeles, boarded a plane at LAX airport, and flew to Vancouver. He was there for six months, then "arranged to get a passport." From there he flew to Cancún—he didn't want to fly direct—then headed to Rio de Janeiro, Brazil. He worked as a "broker for seasonal apartments" and met his wife, Marcia. They were together for three years when she became pregnant with his son, John Paul.

Blatt would end his direct examination by asking, "At any time, any time, did you ever request or order Mr. Hoyt to hurt Nick?" Hollywood aggressively answered, "Never." He would continue to state how "I feel terrible for the Markowitz family. I feel terrible for all the families involved in this ordeal. And I feel terrible that people would think that of me, that I would do something like that."

And then, as Susan Markowitz watched, he took a final sip from the Smartwater.

But Hollywood wasn't done with the questioning. The court took a break. And in ten minutes, it would be prosecuting attorney Joshua Lynn's turn at the cross-examination.

And Susan? From that day forward, she could never bring herself to drink Smartwater again.

Chapter 29

CROSS-EXAMINATION

"HOW DO YOU FEEL RIGHT NOW?" THAT WAS JOSHUA Lynn's first question to Hollywood. "Remember you said you felt terrible?" he would remind the defendant.

He would then cut straight to the point. "Do you believe that you are guilty of anything with respect to Nick Markowitz?" To which Hollywood replied, "Not taking him home." Lynn would get out of him that he felt bad for pinning Nick up against the tree and "taking him to Santa Barbara." Hollywood acknowledged the kidnapping, but that was as far as his accountability would go. Hollywood even suggested that Nick was the more intimidating individual because of his height advantage.

Hollywood purposely referred to Nick in the present tense when Lynn asked, "He was considerably taller, wasn't he?" Hollywood responded, "Yes, he is." Lynn had to remind him, "*Was*, right? He *was* a lot taller than you. . . ."

Though others testified that Hollywood ordered the white van to stop when he saw Nick, on the stand Hollywood couldn't remember who gave the command. He said it could have been Skidmore who said, "That's Ben's brother." However, Skidmore never even knew Ben had a brother. Lynn would ask, "Can you tell me why it is that Rugge would stop the van upon seeing Nick Markowitz if it wasn't by your order?"

Hollywood would retreat into saying, "It was right after my windows had been broken." He would refer to this reason more than half a dozen times during his testimony, often prefacing his answers with how Ben had broken his windows. Lynn would make a point that Nick had zero connection to Hollywood. He didn't owe him money and he hadn't broken his windows.

Lynn would establish early on that Hollywood was the one calling the shots. He asked Hollywood what decisions he made that day, August 6. And even though it might have seemed innocuous as Hollywood answered about making the call to go to Fiesta, to pick up Brian Affronti, and to pin Nick up against the tree, Lynn was laying the groundwork for Hollywood as the decision maker to have Nick murdered.

Hollywood would scramble with Lynn's questions regarding his involvement, often prefacing his response by stating his regret as opposed to directly answering the question.

Hollywood would often contradict himself, stating, "I wasn't using Nick for anything," even though he would ask Nick about his brother's whereabouts, and tell Lynn, "I wanted to confront Ben and end this feud."

Skidmore had already said the intention was to head over to the Markowitzes' to hopefully find Ben or break some of their windows. If Hollywood's true intention that day was to simply pick up Brian Affronti and head to Santa Barbara, why did he have Rugge come down at all? Why not just meet Rugge up at Fiesta?

Hollywood testified that Skidmore punched Nick and "ushered" him into the van. Hollywood would also counter what Chas Saulsbury testified to about there being guns in the white van. Skidmore stated that at the time, there was at least an AR-15.

Lynn would find it convenient that Hollywood's memory was better during direct examination than during cross-examination. "Can you picture sitting in the van right now; can you picture sitting in the van on the way to Brian Affronti's house?" Hollywood would answer no. "So what memory are you testifying from?"

Though Hollywood would say Nick was always free to go, Lynn would point out that he never once said, "Go ahead. That was a stupid thing, whatever, it's over. Go ahead and leave." In fact, there was never any talk of letting Nick go. Hollywood admitted he never "ordered" anybody to let Nick go.

Hollywood made the bizarre statement that the kidnapping had ended once Nick was *inside the van*. Did he think Nick was just along for the ride at this point? He would state, "We started driving and he was with us." Lynn dug deeper: "If Nick wasn't being held captive, but he's in the van with you . . . tell me what Nick's options were at that time?" Lynn wanted to know what Nick could have done to free himself. Hollywood would shift the responsibility onto Nick, and how this fifteen-year-old could have said, "Let me out right here."

Hollywood would try and claim that because Nick wasn't in any restraints, that that meant he wasn't being held captive. Lynn finally got Hollywood to agree that Nick was being held against his will.

Regarding Nick's pager going off, Lynn would ask Hollywood if he remembered saying, "Is that your fucking brother Ben calling?" Hollywood said he never said that. Lynn would fire back, "Is there something about this van ride that isn't memorable to you? Is there something . . . that's happened that caused you to forget what happened in the van?"

Lynn would bring up the point again and again that if Nick was of no use to Hollywood contacting Ben, then why have Nick around at all? Why not let him go? Hollywood fell back on stating that there was never a plan. It was impulsive. Just as it was up to Nick to decide when he was free to go.

Hollywood wouldn't recall ever putting Nick's wallet or pager on the dash right in front of him. Hollywood wouldn't recall the ring he took from Nick and that Rugge had him return.

Once at Richard Hoeflinger's, Hollywood stated that he wasn't "horrified" that Nick's hands and feet were taped. Lynn would counter, "You weren't horrified at a fifteen-year-old in a stranger's home who was bound in the bedroom?"

Hollywood said Skidmore was being aggressive, that he ordered Skidmore to remove the tape. He said he was trying to de-escalate the situation because of Skidmore's aggression, never once mentioning that Affronti had asked to leave because he had a date. He made it seem like he was the one who sent Affronti and Skidmore home.

Again, Lynn pressed Hollywood regarding Nick's choices in the matter. "You didn't give him a phone and say, 'Call home'?" Or give him "fifty bucks. 'Get yourself home'?"

Lynn would ask if Nick's murder was the most significant event in the entire episode of events. Hollywood answered, "I'd say it's a terrible, horrible event. Not a significant—I mean, it's a horrible event." Lynn would counter, "Tell me what was worse? Was there a worse event during this whole episode?" Finally Hollywood would answer that there wasn't, putting his broken windows, his need to sell his home, his need to find a condo, and his desire to attend Fiesta as secondary.

Again, when Lynn asked why he didn't let Nick go back to Los Angeles with Skidmore and Affronti, Hollywood mentioned how he was sidetracked, and those million things took precedence. According to Hollywood's testimony, "And, you know, we had ordered food."

Hollywood said that he had been making phone calls to get a ride home, yet when he secured a ride, Nick was never offered one home. And with that, day one finally came to a close.

Though it went against the judge's orders, Susan Markowitz would be consoled by a few witnesses. "They weren't legally allowed to approach us," but that didn't stop Chas Saulsbury. "Chas met us off to the side." He "showed the largest amount of remorse." During his testimony, Chas had stated that his dog had been mysteriously poisoned, maybe as a threat against taking the stand. After Chas met with Susan off to the side, she expressed her condolences and believed it could only have been Hollywood who ordered the poisoning. "I don't know who could possibly be involved in that other than the original scum who took my son's life."

Before questioning resumed on day two of Hollywood's cross-examination, Judge Brian Hill met with the attorneys off the record and away from the jury.

Lynn wanted to make a request of the court regarding one of Hollywood's defense lawyers. "The next time that Mr. Kessel loudly in an open court calls me a dickhead or several other names that I could think of, I would appreciate if the court would address it. And if Mr. Kessel wants to object to that, I'll put somebody on the stand right now to talk about the three instances."

Blatt would stipulate to having Hollywood's leg shackles removed while testifying.

This set the tone for the day.

Back on the record, Lynn resumed. He opened up with Hollywood worrying more about getting himself home to Los Angeles than Nick. "Is it fair to conclude . . . that at least at the time that you decided to go home it was more important to you to do that than to bring Nick back with you?" Hollywood answered that he didn't see any order of importance of plans. As far as Hollywood was concerned, Nick was "free to go" after he left Hoeflinger's.

Lynn had to remind the defendant that he never vocalized, "Nick, you're free to go."

The district attorney would bring up other witnesses' testimony—those who were told that Nick wasn't allowed to use the phone, who were told not to disclose to Nick that he was in Santa Barbara. Even though Hollywood would deny saying it, Lynn asked him why he said Nick was to stay until Ben could be found.

Returning to Nick's pager, Hollywood would say he didn't know who paged Nick, even though Nick said it was his mother. Again, Hollywood never let him call home.

Lynn pressed him again about him kidnapping Nick "in an irrational effort to confront Ben." But Hollywood didn't need Nick to find Ben. He had been to Ben's place with Ryan Hoyt, waiting in front of his apartment. So what was the real reason he abducted Nick?

Lynn pointed out, "In your effort to de-escalate, you didn't take Nick, you just gave the van to Skidmore and Affronti?" When another one of Hollywood's friends finally showed up to get him, he again passed up the chance to bring Nick home. Lynn then pressed further, asking why he would need a ride at all. Why not just go back to LA with Skidmore and Affronti? Hollywood couldn't remember. Lynn pressed, "Mr. Hollywood, if you say you don't remember, do you believe that that will just absolve you from the need to answer the question?"

Lynn would often back Hollywood into a corner with his questioning. Again, Hollywood would contradict himself. He would say he couldn't remember certain witnesses' testimony, but then, after Lynn refreshed his memory, he would vehemently dismiss the exact testimony he couldn't recall. Or as Lynn put it, "How would you know if you don't remember?"

But Lynn continued to play the long game, pointing out that it was interesting that Hollywood couldn't remember his exact words or was fuzzy the majority of the time. Yet when a witness said something damning against him, he had *instant recall* and denied he'd ever said it.

Hollywood, who constantly wiped his brow, was adamant that Nick was always free to go "as far as I was concerned." Lynn countered by asking him, "How was he made aware of his freedom?" Hollywood stammered through the answer, before Lynn followed up, "So it was up to Nick to figure out when and if he could leave?" Essentially, this fifteen-year-old was somehow *now in charge* of his own kidnapping and release. Lynn would then ask, "Mr. Hollywood, was this just an unplanned vacation that Nick should have been thanking you for?"

Questioning Hollywood about the night of the abduction, Lynn would bring Hollywood's utter disregard to the surface: "At the time that you were eating that burrito, were you thinking that perhaps Nick Markowitz needed a ride back to Los Angeles to be with his family?"

Again, Hollywood's memory failed him. "I can't remember what I was thinking."

Lynn attempted to find out who supplied Hollywood with his weed. "Well," Hollywood answered, "people who grow marijuana." He couldn't recall names. He was certain, though, that he never thought about calling the police after feeling threatened by Ben Markowitz.

Lynn would ask why Hollywood—who had just been in Santa Barbara the day before the abduction—wanted to bring Jesse Rugge back to Los Angeles to collect on Ben's drug debt. Whoever said that, Hollywood testified, they must have heard it wrong.

Lynn pointed out that the specific reason tape was around the handle of the TEC-9 was to make it harder to pull fingerprints.

He would throw in quick non sequiturs to keep Hollywood scrambling. He would ask about Hollywood going to the gun range to fire the TEC-9 and then in the next sentence ask him if he agreed that Nick would be alive today if he hadn't "taken" him in the van.

Hollywood repeatedly stated there was "nothing out of the ordinary" happening following Nick's abduction. Lynn would fire back, "Other than an uninvited fifteen-year-old brought to a houseful of strangers a hundred miles from his home, right?"

Lynn kept pressing, "Did you say to Nick he'll be home in a couple of days?" Hollywood denied it. Lynn followed, "So you don't know where Mr. Affronti may have gotten that information?" And that was how the day went, Hollywood's memory going back and forth from never recalling to total recall when it only hurt his case.

Hollywood couldn't recall whether he'd ever asked Rugge if Nick had been let go, though he did remember the five hundred dollars he was owed by Rugge. He couldn't recall Rugge pleading with him to get Nick because, "I can't have Nick at my parents'."

Hollywood had tons of plans during those two and a half days. He wanted to sell his house, find a condo, and fix his windows. One plan he never made, as Lynn pointed out, was to return Nick back home.

Hollywood said he asked Nick at one point while they were at Jesse Rugge's if he wanted to go home. He stated that Nick said, "No, I'm cool." Lynn would press him, "Did it surprise you that Nick Markowitz, whom you had pinned against a tree and put in a van the day before and brought one hundred miles from his home, didn't want to hop in a car with you, did that surprise you?"

Hollywood denied ever offering Rugge two thousand dollars to kill Nick. He denied ever joking that he wanted to put Nick in the trunk of a car and then head to dinner. Again, whoever stated anything against him "simply has that wrong," Lynn would sarcastically opine.

Lynn would question Hollywood about how he'd gone to his attorney, Stephen Hogg, for advice about Nick's abduction. Apparently, life in prison for kidnapping for ransom wasn't a concern to Hollywood that he felt he needed to tell Rugge. Hollywood stated that Nick was in no danger. Lynn would ask, "And the non-danger with Rugge is based on the zero phone calls on August seventh?"

Lynn would press and ask why Hollywood simply didn't postpone his dinner at the Outback Steakhouse instead of tasking Hoyt, a guy he didn't trust and deemed unreliable, to pick up Nick.

Even though Hollywood—only fifteen minutes away from Casey Sheehan's—would stop at a pay phone to call Rugge after he picked up Hoyt in Casey Sheehan's car from his own house, he never once thought he needed to page anyone to see if Nick had actually been returned or if Hoyt had found the Lemon Tree Inn.

Lynn couldn't ask Hollywood about the events of August 9. Hollywood had complete and total memory loss of that day apart from a phone call with Hoyt.

After having enough of Hollywood's memory loss, Lynn finally asked, "And do you feel if you just say you don't remember that I'll stop asking?" He would jest at Hollywood's "full blackout mode."

Lynn would then press him with a series of questions regarding Hoyt:

"Right now, to this day, does Ryan Hoyt owe you money?"

"I wouldn't—I'm not concerned with—if Hoyt owes me money or not."

"I didn't ask you that."

"I think that's—"

"Mr. Hollywood, does Ryan Hoyt owe you money right now or not?"

"I don't know how to answer that question."

"Yes or no."

"I don't—I don't know how to answer that question, sir."

"That's because you paid him for a job well done, didn't you?"

Hollywood's Freudian slip was just a few questions away: he would answer a question he was never asked. "I don't think a hundred or two hundred dollars is a significant amount enough to kill somebody." Lynn would reply, "Why did you just say that? Did I ask you a question about killing somebody?"

Hollywood kept trying to distance himself from having any part in Nick's death. Lynn wasn't buying it and had had enough: "If the murder of an innocent fifteen-year-old boy didn't cause you to go to the police, can you tell us what would?"

Regarding Ryan Hoyt's birthday party the night after Nick was killed: "Why during that period of time . . . were you offering money for Ben Markowitz to be harmed?"

Lynn would question him about heading to Palm Springs, Vegas, Colorado, then back to Los Angeles, where he hid out in the Mojave Desert before heading to Canada, then Brazil. On his ventures from Colorado back to Los Angeles, Hollywood would state he was praying and asking God for help. Lynn wouldn't let him off that easily. "You didn't say you were asking for God to help Nick or his family, did you?" He quickly followed up with, "This was about you, wasn't it, you were praying for yourself because you knew you were in a world of trouble."

Lynn would press Hollywood as to whether he remembered writing to somebody that he thought it was funny "that they were teargassing John Roberts's house while you were a hundred miles away drinking a cold Coors Light?"

Hollywood would answer one question with clarity, that he chose Brazil based on the movie *Blame It on Rio*, because Canada had been "freezing cold and I was miserable."

Lynn wanted to know if Hollywood could recall something he said to the detectives in the Santa Barbara County Sheriff's Office after being apprehended. "Do you remember telling them how disappointed your father would be at the way you were caught?" And, sticking to the theme of his entire cross-examination, *he did not*.

Closing arguments would follow.

Chapter 30

A MOTHER REMEMBERS

SUSAN MARKOWITZ WOULD SPEND COUNTLESS hours rereading the journal entries she shared with Nick. She was thankful she'd told him to stop writing in pencil because she was worried his entries would fade.

Susan would think back and smile at certain memories. One was Nick's childhood nickname, originating from his habit of cleaning his nose with a finger. In a play on words, she would joke and call him, "No PickNick." She thought back to the day they were running late for school and "Nick was wearing orange sweats and a green turtleneck, for God's sake." She was sure he was "making fun of me now."

She reread a particular entry, dated October 22, 1992:

Thanks for the letter, Mom. By the way, my day was pretty good and bad, but it will get better. I am really glad you got me this book. I think this will be fun and I really, really like my new desk. Please write back.

For Susan, it wasn't just the content of the entries; it was the passion with which they were written. "It's so sad to go back in time and see his pain as a little kid. You wouldn't know that if you wouldn't have written it down."

Dear Mom, today I was made fun of from [four people]. They called me a jerk and an idiot and a fool. They say my bike sucks. I don't think it does but needs a new seat, new gears, new brakes, new everything. What did I do wrong? Well, I'm glad I have you to talk to cause I have no one else, not even my best friend. . . . I don't know what to do. Please wake up early before dad, and talk to me please. Well, I've got to go now. I love you. Your son, Nick.

Susan couldn't wait. She had to wake him right then. They discussed his entry, but didn't leave it at that. Susan would write her own reply:

Dear Nicholas, I enjoyed our talk. I hope you understand what I was trying to tell you—the most important thing for you to remember is you didn't do anything wrong. Sometimes people get embarrassed or try to change the subject by doing harmful things which is wrong, but unfortunately a part of growing up.

* * *

Though Nick's pager had been discarded on the side of the road, Susan saw things that made her think that Nick had found a way to communicate with her. "I live up against the mountains, and I see hawks and falcons, and we used to have memories of those while taking him to school. I feel like he's still here." She wouldn't go as far as to say he was speaking to her in her dreams. "You can't live for those type of things. You have to take it as they come."

Chapter 31

CLOSING ARGUMENTS

JUNE 30, 2009. EIGHT DAYS AFTER HOLLYWOOD'S questioning had commenced.

A homicide during the commission of a kidnapping. This was the first point Lynn wanted to remind the jury about. The kidnapping didn't end when Hollywood left Hoeflinger's house on the sixth. No, it ended with Nick's death. To the prosecution, this was one continuous transaction. On Hollywood's orders. Which was why Lynn stated in his opening argument that it was as if Hollywood pulled the trigger himself. Just because he wasn't present for the first-degree murder, that didn't exonerate him from being convicted of it. "Mr. Hollywood should be a convicted kidnapper and child murderer and there's no doubt about it."

The second point: "This case is about Nick Markowitz, it's not about Jesse Hollywood. Jesse Hollywood is still alive, he's sitting right there. This case is about Nick and Nick's story and what happened to him."

Lynn reminded the jury, "Hollywood was always having somebody else go do deeds for him." He called Hollywood out for not being a "gun guy," yet cited no less than four different guns he had in his possession.

Lynn pointed out that during direct examination with his own attorney, Hollywood answered questions beautifully. But on cross-examination? He remembered "all but that which gets him in trouble." He made the point that every time someone was doing something on behalf of Hollywood, Hollywood himself was somewhere eating. Hollywood never said a negative thing about himself. He did, however, repeat "regretting this and regretting that," regardless of whether the question asked for it.

Lynn went on to state that if this whole dispute were singularly based on Ben Markowitz's debt, Jeff Markowitz would have paid it. He pointed out again how Jeff had paid Ben's rent while Ben was living with Hollywood. No, this murder was done to make a point: *You don't fuck with me.*

Lynn stressed that Chas Saulsbury had no motive to make up any of his witness testimony, including his testifying at trial (though not in an earlier proceeding) that Hollywood had claimed that Hogg told him that if he wasn't going to call the police, he "needed to dig a deep hole." (Hogg reportedly denied having said this; he also reportedly said he didn't have enough information to call the police himself.)

Lynn pointed out the absurdity of Rugge stopping the van

independent of Hollywood's orders, as Hollywood tried to minimize the kidnapping. Never mind the fact that once Nick was
in the van, Lynn stated that Hollywood screamed at him, "Your
brother is going to pay me my money." According to Lynn, "I
don't have any better way to explain why Nick was kidnapped
than out of Hollywood's mouth himself."

Lynn reminded the jury how Hollywood kept saying Nick was
free to go. *But go where?* Especially in a moving van. Once Nick
stated that he didn't know where they could find Ben, Hollywood
didn't open the door or pull off to the side of the road. No, he
continued on. Lynn asserted, "This is a kidnap for ransom."

As far as the kidnapping being a continuous transaction,
Lynn repeated how Affronti told Nick "don't do anything stupid."
For the next three days, Nick did just that. Until it ended his life.
Even though Affronti had a cell phone, Nick wasn't even allowed
to call his mother, who was desperately paging him.

Evidence indicated that Hollywood did indeed intend to keep
Nick until Ben could be found and he could collect his debt. On
day one of the kidnapping, Hollywood told Nick, "Just tell your
parents you were gone for a couple of days." It went on three
days. As Lynn pointed out, "Home isn't where he went."

Hollywood didn't remember the majority of witnesses who
testified, but according to Lynn, "They sure remember him." He
even brought up the irony of the *Twilight Zone* sign above the
closet in Hoeflinger's room, where Nick was initially almost held.

It made no sense for Hollywood to find a ride home when
he had his own van right outside, according to Lynn. Lynn

stressed that Hollywood was "on an island with his testimony" in comparison to every other witness, who corroborated the facts in the case—independently, without ever having spoken to one another, and speaking to the police separately.

Lynn reminded the jury that this case was about Nick. "In his fifteen-year-old mind, he believes he needs to do this for his brother." Stay put and not cause a confrontation.

And when Hollywood left Hoeflinger's? Lynn stated, "You don't get to extricate yourself from the crimes you committed by simply walking out the door."

Lynn stressed that witnesses chose not to call the police because they were more scared of what Hollywood would do to them than what would happen to Nick if they didn't.

Hollywood had no responsibility to the kidnapped victim, "but he had a responsibility to his windows." A responsibility to feed himself a burrito when he returned to Los Angeles, to buy a new car, to take his girlfriend to dinner on her birthday. Hollywood's priorities were "horrifying." And Nick was never one of them. "It's why he's dead."

Hollywood was guilty of aiding and abetting, according to Lynn. He provided the car for Hoyt to get to the Lemon Tree, provided the gun, the incentive of forgiving his debt, and the order. It made no difference whether he was the shooter. "Ask yourself," Lynn told the jury. "How did Hoyt even know Nick Markowitz was kidnapped?"

On August 8, Nick was still complying, Lynn argued. Why would he be asked if he would go to the police once released?

"And this is the day that Nick is going to be murdered, he just doesn't know it yet."

One of the saddest facts that Lynn emphasized was that Hollywood's own attorney never notified the police. Instead he spoke to Jack Hollywood.

As far as fleeing, Lynn reminded the jury that Hollywood's intent was to hit the road before Nick was killed, "because he wants to make sure everybody else is on the hook for this killing instead of him."

Incredibly, Lynn pointed out, there was no effort to return Ben Markowitz's four attempts to call Hollywood, because Hollywood already knew Nick was dead. He didn't even ask Hoyt, "Well, where is the TEC-9?" Hollywood believed that Nick's kidnapping wouldn't "up the ante" for Ben. Did Hollywood forget about the note reading, "Take this off Ben's debt" at the restaurant, and how that sent Ben off the edge?

Lynn reminded the court that Sheehan was told by Hoyt, "Hey, the debt to Hollywood's paid." When Sheehan confronted Hollywood about the murder, Hollywood didn't react with surprise or horror. No, as Lynn quoted Sheehan, Hollywood stated, "Don't worry about it." This countered Hollywood's testimony about how he never could have foreseen this murder happening.

As far as Hoyt and Hollywood arguing at Hoyt's birthday party, Lynn stressed that Hollywood wasn't upset that Hoyt murdered Nick. No, he was pissed that Hoyt left the gun at the crime scene and involved a total stranger to him, Graham Pressley.

Lynn reminded the jury once again about Hollywood's selective memory. "He remembers Palm Springs with his mom, and the lunch before with mom." He also remembered he got his new car washed. But he never mentioned Nick. "He has a fantastic memory for those things that don't get him in trouble."

Hollywood then "visited this nightmare upon Chas Saulsbury." According to Lynn, "He went and told people half-truths and partial stories about what was going on in his life and what happened to him so that they would help him. And he [Hollywood] was the Colorado hot potato."

Lynn wanted the jury to ask, "What's in it for Chas?" to lie about his testimony. He had information that could only have come from Hollywood, seeing it wasn't printed in any papers. "How does he know [that] Hoyt says [to] the group, 'I'll do it'?" Chas pointed out that Hollywood told him, "Who the fuck is this kid?" regarding Graham Pressley. "If Hollywood had nothing to do with the murder . . . why does he care who Graham Pressley is or why he was there?" If Hollywood had nothing to hide, according to Lynn, why would he need to say, "I'd started a new life for myself," when he was in Brazil? Why run if you're innocent?

Lynn was adamant that the jury ask themselves, "What is Hoyt's independent motive? I have no clue." Lynn challenged the defense to answer the question, knowing they couldn't because "their client is the motive for Hoyt murdering Nick Markowitz. Even Hollywood can't think of a reason." Lynn reminded the jury that Ben Markowitz had zero beef with Hoyt, so it couldn't be him.

Lynn brought back the theme of why everyone was here and

quoted Hollywood, "Our world became everybody's world." Lynn said he didn't know what that meant, but it was a "very good window into this sort of egomaniacal personality that he has." Hollywood didn't make it Nick's world. "This is Hollywood's world."

Lynn would show the jury a picture of Nick before he was kidnapped and contrast it to what he looked like after he was murdered, "bound behind the back, unburied from his grave." He would show the picture of Jeff Markowitz's ring that Hollywood didn't recall taking before Rugge had him return it.

Lynn ended by using Hollywood's own terminology against him. "I would urge you to *usher* Jesse Hollywood into his new status as a convicted kidnapper, a convicted child murderer . . . it's time. Convict him."

Hollywood's defense attorney, Alex Kessel, spoke first, followed by Blatt. He would state that the theme of this trial was parallel to the movie *Get Shorty*, calling it *Get Hollywood*. He said that every witness had been corrupted by the movie *Alpha Dog* and asserted that it was impossible for them not to have seen it.

Kessel would appeal to the jury not to be swayed by the crime scene photos. "You can't fill the voids of the People's case with pictures of Nick Markowitz in the grave." But what exactly were those voids? Lynn cited specific lines from testimony. Kessel, not being a gun expert, would make the confusing and unsubstantiated claim that "the TEC-9 is not the type of gun that you want to kill one person with."

As day two of closing arguments began—and before the jury

was brought in—Kessel would bring to the court's attention how unsuitable it was for Nick's parents to be crying at the crime scene photos, that the emotions of the mother and father of a murdered child would automatically influence the jury. Lynn would interject, "I suppose Mr. Kessel is now going to argue with the jurors that were crying and say that they should be thrown off as well."

Judge Hill would remind the audience to temper any emotions, but the way Kessel attributed an agenda behind the Markowitzes' crying could be seen as a stretch. Kessel even tried to downplay how much time had passed since Nick's death calling it a few years. Jeff Markowitz was vehement in reminding the defense attorneys that "it's been nine years." That prompted the judge to ask him to leave the audience.

Instead of citing testimony, which the jury would use as evidence, Kessel admonished Lynn for not bringing in particular witnesses. Kessel was suggesting that the reason Lynn chose not to was because it would hurt or contradict the State's narrative. As far as the Ecstasy dealer in San Diego who Ben Markowitz knew, Kessel would say, "Go down and bring him up as a witness. Have him tell you." He wanted to distance Hollywood from having someone collect a debt.

Kessel would remind the jury that Nick "is closer to sixteen than he is fifteen." And just like Hollywood, he was speaking about Nick in the present tense, adding that small fact of his upcoming September birthday. Was this to make Nick appear a more mature murder victim?

Kessel argued that Nick was "in his element." Smoking, drinking, again making the statement without any corroboration from a witness that "he loves smoking. That's what he does." Kessel would speculate that when Nick was at Rugge's, he didn't want to call home. He even spoke on Nick's behalf: "Well, Mom, I was in my element. I was smoking weed and doing drugs and having fun and drinking." He would say Nick was "enjoying himself." How did Kessel know exactly what Nick was thinking?

Kessel tried to discredit Graham Pressley's testimony, calling him a "convicted felon." He would state that because he was an accomplice, the "accomplice has motives to lie." With an accomplice, you need another witness to corroborate his testimony. If Graham Pressley testified that Hollywood offered Jesse Rugge two thousand dollars to murder Nick, why not bring in Rugge to corroborate it? "Where is Jesse Rugge?" Kessel would point out, "He was number seventy-four on their witness list." Kessel would spend time speculating on the fictional testimony of witnesses who weren't there rather than citing those who were. "He's a logical and critical witness and they won't call him. And don't let them tell you we can call him, that's not right. They have the burden."

Kessel would later refer to Chas Saulsbury as "the human bong." After lunch, when it was Blatt's turn, he would continue lambasting Saulsbury, who "obviously appears to have some mental problems."

Blatt wouldn't serve only the witnesses with backhanded comments. He would do the same with Lynn and the other state prosecutor, Hans Almgren. "I'm sure they're very good persons.

They're dedicated public servants. And the analysis that I give is not a personal attack. They cannot help if the majority of their witnesses are perjurers. They cannot help if many of these individuals seem to have some type of permanent damage to their brains due to constant marijuana use."

Blatt continued to bleat about the witnesses who were not present. He wondered why Ben Markowitz's fiancée at the time wasn't brought in to talk about what Hollywood said about taking money off Ben's debt.

He would comment on the absence of the investigating officer. "How do you have a murder case of this magnitude without even bringing an investigating officer to develop how the case began?"

Instead of reiterating evidence and testimony, Blatt informed the jury about Jesse Hollywood's name. "Hollywood is an Irish name. Jesse and James are Biblical names." Was his ethnicity and origin of his middle name supposed to factor into determining whether he would be convicted of first-degree murder?

Picking up where Kessel left off, Blatt would once again address *Alpha Dog*. "This is the first time . . . in our Anglo American history where the movie comes out before the trial." Was Blatt presuming the nine women and three men were judging their client strictly on the movie as opposed to the last seven weeks of trial?

Blatt would take his shots at Ben Markowitz also. "You've got to lower yourself as a two-year-old to go out and break somebody's windows."

What was Blatt's strategy in bringing up Hollywood's perfect credit for a second time? "How many individuals do you know have a seven fifty to eight hundred FICO score . . . at twenty years old?"

Blatt would state that Hoyt killed Nick for acceptance. He lied about being a Navy SEAL. Lied about being a model. He was desperate. "I need to be somebody." He would leave out the testimony that Hoyt also wanted to clear his debt by doing something more than just sanding down Hollywood's hot tub.

Blatt would never state why Hollywood didn't simply let Nick go when Nick was of no use in finding Ben. Instead Blatt would claim his client's rationale was, "You don't know where he is. All right, all right. I'm angry, but we're going to still run away to Fiesta."

If Blatt was trying to distance his client from seeing Nick as a problem, he didn't do Hollywood a service by speculating on Hoyt's behalf, "I've just taken care of your problem. I've done the ultimate for you."

Blatt would also try and make the case that Hollywood would now have to kill every single witness who was involved in this matter if he truly wanted Nick murdered.

Lynn would have the last opportunity to speak per guidelines during closing arguments. It was his burden to show proof. He would point out that the defense had the exact same subpoena powers as the State. They could have called any witness also.

As far as Hoyt, he would ask the jury, "Does this guy look like an independent thinker to you?"

He would hit home the fact that Hollywood had a good reason to run. "It's because he was guilty as sin and he knew he was going to jail for life."

Lynn didn't have to speculate on the evidence like the defense. He told the jury he used 178 slides and 78 citations to back up his closing argument.

He reminded the jury how Ben Markowitz had testified that he didn't care if he lived or died now that his brother was dead, and how he felt responsible. Contrast that to Jesse Hollywood, who fled town and threw everybody else under the bus.

When it came to addressing the crime scene photos that the defense was so worried about—and the way they would evoke emotion—Lynn would state they were shown for one single reason. To show how Hollywood didn't care enough about Nick to even remember he took his ring.

Lastly, he would reiterate, "Nick was not free to leave in his own mind." If Hollywood didn't tell Nick he could leave, then who else was going to? "Is it up to Miss [Natasha] Adams to set him free?"

Lynn would implore the jury to convict Hollywood. The jury was then sequestered for deliberation. How long would they take? An hour, a day, a month? No one knew.

Chapter 32

VERDICT

JESSE JAMES HOLLYWOOD WAS FOUND GUILTY OF
kidnapping and first-degree murder on July 8, 2009. The jury,
after four days of deliberation, did not believe the kidnapping
was done for ransom or extortion. However, jurors did believe
Hollywood supplied Hoyt with the TEC-9. This "special circum-
stance," in the language of the law, made the mastermind behind
the murder subject to the death penalty.

A poignant testament that this *was* always about Nick and not
about Hollywood, as Lynn stated, took place on break during
closing arguments. Juror number one, who was on a breathing
machine, was having difficulty catching her breath. At one point
a deputy informed Judge Hill that she was going to be trans-
ported to the hospital. But then the latest word came in that she
insisted on remaining as a juror.

Even though Judge Hill's preference was to dismiss her, he allowed her to have her say. He asked if it was true that she'd been having respiratory problems "in the last thirty or forty minutes."

She was adamant about continuing on. "I think I told you I had that esophageal cancer and my lungs collapsed, and once in a while I still need my oxygen. I was a little winded this morning. I probably shouldn't have taken it out." She stated that the room had started spinning. Judge Hill inquired whether the reinsertion of the device meant she was now feeling more comfortable.

"I'm a tough old bird," she answered. She would state how embarrassed she was and let the court know she "was good to go."

Judge Hill would reply, "You're good to go. You're a tough old bird."

This wasn't about her. Indeed, this was about Nick.

Six days after he was found guilty, Jesse Hollywood would receive a life sentence without the possibility of parole. Detective Valencia, the man who didn't exist for eight months, was there at the sentencing. But Hollywood didn't recognize the person who had tracked him down in Brazil. And for good reason. Valencia had cut off his sixteen-inch braid, once again donating it to kids suffering from cancer.

In 2010, Judge Brian Hill upheld Hollywood's life sentence. "It has been a very long ten years," Susan Markowitz would inform the *Santa Barbara Independent*. However, Judge Hill had not allowed her to read her Victim Impact Statement, describing what the loss of her son had done to her and her family. "I am still in disbelief. I wish I could have told my story." But Judge Hill's denial of Susan's Impact Statement was correct in the eyes of the court. After the defense filed various motions for a retrial, Judge Hill only had the power to uphold the life sentence or grant a retrial. He denied the motions, which meant the Impact Statement would not have had any influence on the life sentence.

However, Susan did end up telling her side of the story, penning a book from her point of view about Nick, entitled *My Stolen Son*.

Looking back at the trial, Susan Markowitz says of Hollywood, "He hid out for five years. Why would you hide out if you were not guilty?" She believes he couldn't live behind the excuse that he was afraid of being shot on sight. Couldn't he simply call his lawyer and arrange to peacefully turn himself over to authorities?

Susan fervently believes that if marijuana had been legalized, "my son would be alive today." She adds, "You don't read in the paper or see on the news how someone was stoned and out shooting." Though she doesn't smoke, she believes it's safer than alcohol. Marijuana is "possibly the number one cancer cure. I'm not very political, but something seems a little backward sixteen years after the death of my son, and I wonder what's going on." One example: according to the FBI, in 2014 nearly 620,000 people were arrested for simple marijuana possession across the United States.

Susan might have had to sit through more court hearings than she could ever have imagined. That doesn't stop her from welcoming one more trial. "The finale," as she calls it. "His *father's*," referring to Jack Hollywood standing trial for his role in Nick's murder. For Susan, "that's the only justice that is incomplete. He could have saved so many lives." In regard to Jesse Hollywood's life sentence and his father, she believes, "He killed his son. What kind of person is that?" She believes Jack's influence could have determined the decision to murder Nick. "*Do it.* That's how I think it happened."

However, regarding Jesse Hollywood's life sentence, she feels, "That did not bring me pleasure, knowing that *someone else's son is going to be murdered.*"

There were multiple attempts to correspond with Jesse James Hollywood to obtain his input on the specific themes found in this book:

Show me your friends and I'll show you your future

Choices and consequences

Accountability

It's never too late to write your own ending

How can we avoid the next innocent teen from being murdered?

Jesse Hollywood was not interested in discussing these themes. Instead he expressed his thoughts in a letter written in December 2015.

I will reiterate myself. I am already working on a project and have been for the last 5 years. . . This is the only real story.

If you or [your agent] is interested in helping me accomplish
that I may be willing to help you. Of course, we'd have to
come to a mutual agreement that would benefit us both.

Those terms were not agreed to and all correspondence eventually ceased. He is currently serving his time at Calipatria State Prison.

Attempts were also made to reach out to Ryan Hoyt on death
row in San Quentin. The intent was to ascertain his input regarding the same themes. This was his written response in a letter
dated November 5, 2015.

Thank you for your letter and interest in, not just my case,
but in me. I'm actually sorry that I'm writing you to tell you
that I'm not interested. Whether it was the idiots who made
the movie or any of the other ones, they always just assumed
I'd want to be involved without really caring about what I've
[had] to deal with here.

As a rule I don't write people trying to make money off
of other people's misery. I'm not saying that's what you're
doing. Clearly, it's not. But I cannot make exceptions.
Authors, media, Police. In my experience they've become
the same thing.

However, I really appreciated your approach. And the way
you got at me. I wish you the best of luck on your project,
but I have to decline any involvement.

Thank you for your interest.

—Ryan

Chapter 33

FINDING STRENGTH

UP UNTIL A FEW YEARS AGO, SUSAN WOULD CALL HIS voice mail just to hear her son's voice. And up until a few years ago, she would regularly visit his grave. Lately, she's given herself some distance.

"I find that for the past year and a half . . . when I go to Nick's grave I become angry, and I don't want to become angry. I just don't want to lower myself to the level of the people that took him and become angry and maybe act out of a spontaneous moment within anger because that's how things usually happen. Or [through] fear. So I just avoid tapping into that possible anger."

She might not have recently visited Nick's grave, but she does hold him close in other ways. To this day, she carries a keepsake from Nick.

"I wear the ring that he bought me for Mother's Day. It's

getting very, *very* thin. It used to be inscribed, 'Love, Nick.'" Nick was ten when he bought it for her. "It was this *itty-bitty* little sapphire with a gold band. It's his birthstone. Within the past couple of years I put it on a chain, because I'm afraid that it's going to break and I will lose it. So that is probably the most heartfelt gift piece of jewelry that I have. I certainly hope nobody decides it's worth killing me over," she says, demonstrating the depths of her wounds. "They can have the chain. They can have the other stuff. But don't take my *itty-bitty* sapphire ring."

Susan hasn't always had the ability to deal with her pain and heartache in a positive way. In fact, it's easier for her to recall which prescriptions she *wasn't* on. "2010 is when I took myself off all medications." She explains how mixing two different anti-depressants caused her to feel even more suicidal. Not to mention that she was "taking extra pills that I didn't necessarily need and drinking." She recalls a specific moment when she felt like taking her own life. She had broken the mirror of her compact and tried to slit her wrists with a shard of glass. "This is so not me, but that is what depression will do to you. And that's why when you are traumatized, it's important that everyone has access to the proper health care and psychiatrists and therapists."

Ironically, something that's been therapeutic for Susan isn't the running away from the pain. It's running to it. There was a time she wanted to make it all disappear. But now? "I don't know if I ever want it to go away, because that would mean Nick would go away, and I *never* want that." She questioned herself at one point, *Have I made it to the other side of grief?* "Never," she says.

"Never ever will I make it to the other side. This is going to be with me until I close my eyes and take my last breath."

Susan did want to make it to the other side of forgiveness when it came to Ben. She recalls the process. "We didn't speak for five years. He had written me a letter asking me for forgiveness, but I didn't comprehend what I read until five years *later*. In 2005 his grandmother, my husband's mother, I think it was her seventy-fifth birthday—we were all invited and I didn't want everybody to be looking at us, [knowing] we weren't getting along, or him not being invited or me not wanting to go because he was invited, or vice versa. So I wrote him a letter asking him to meet me at the cemetery. And we did. Jeff and I and him. It was surprisingly the perfect time—yes, there were tears—but there wasn't a lot of conversation that was needed. It was just me missing him, me knowing that I will always love him, and that Nick would want me to love him."

She hopes Ben will one day be able to forgive himself. "I hope so," she says with a long exhale. "I would not be able to say anything other than that. But I hope so. I feel he will never ever be able to make this right and had he had the opportunity, he would have. I have to support him a hundred percent and I do, and I'm so proud of him."

Just like those cassettes she played for Nick when he was a baby, Susan still finds herself dedicating songs to him. One in particular, "I Hope You Dance," by Lee Ann Womack, was released in March of 2000. Part of the opening verse goes, *And when you get the choice to sit it out or dance, I hope you dance . . . I hope you dance.*

"For it to come on these days—it's 2016—to have it suddenly come on when you're feeling sad or down, it is a sign, and you have to appreciate it and take it for what it is. I had heard it about a month before he was kidnapped, and I didn't know the name of the song, or who sang it at the time, and I was still searching, waiting to hear it again, and it never came on while he was still alive, but it came on after he was kidnapped."

In moments when it's impossible to breathe, Susan understands she has no choice but to persevere. Which is one of the reasons she's open about speaking honestly about her son's life. Her focus crystallizes to, *How can we prevent this from happening to the next innocent fifteen-year-old?*

After all these years, Susan has her own story to tell, her own parable. And no, it might not be *The Giving Tree*, but Nick is very much at its core.

LIFE AFTER

WILLIAM SKIDMORE REFLECTS ON NICK'S MURDER and his role. "I was still in shock. I'm thinking now that I look back at it, and as I'm older, I'm thinking maybe if I was just quiet and didn't say anything, it would just go away." He laughs once, not out of humor but because he's ashamed. A nervous reaction. "I know, stupid thing to think."

As far as reaching out to Susan Markowitz, William is hesitant. He doesn't want to open up old wounds for her. "The thing is, I still think about it all the time. That will never go away." He says that if he did have the opportunity to address Susan, he would tell her, "I'm sorry, tell her . . . a lot of lives were ruined. I know that was her son. If I had lost my son . . . it would be very difficult for me to forgive someone who hurt somebody in my family. I look at all the different reasons—the drugs, age, the time. I pray every day. I know that he was innocent."

He conveys that this doesn't relieve him from his liability. "I wish I wouldn't have been such an immature young man." He admits he was looking for validation in all the wrong places.

If he could go back and talk to his twenty-year-old self, he says, "I would have followed what my parents tried to teach me when I was young and not been a late bloomer. My family's a real close family and I know theirs [Markowitzes] are too. I wish I could go back. I ask God for forgiveness. I pray daily. And I can't change the past. I wish I could. That's one thing that's been with me for a long time. 'If I would have done this . . . if I would have done that . . . ,'" he sheepishly admits. "I was a follower, I was a scared child in a twenty-year-old body trying to be cool, trying to fit in."

If he could address Nick today, William says, "I know he wasn't here as long as he should have been here. One day, we'll all be able to go see him. I just wish it had been different. I wish a lot of the decisions I made in my life could have been different. We all got to face our Maker one day, and I ask for forgiveness every day. That's why I try and better myself every day, better than I was yesterday." He grows silent before adding, "My family—they didn't raise me to be a bully. They raised me to be a productive member of society. That's what I'm trying to do. It's hard because stuff happens in life that just makes you want to quit, and I've learned that I can't quit. With Narcotics Anonymous [NA] I'm learning to love myself, because a lot of the decisions I made in the past, a lot of stuff I do—it hurts me, I know it hurts other people too. . . . It's opening my eyes to a lot of things—every action you do, there's a consequence. There's a reaction. You're not just affecting yourself, you're affecting other people—your family, your parents, people that care for you." He wants to one day visit Lizard's Mouth and privately make amends.

When it comes to Ben Markowitz? "I wish him the best, I really do. We had good times together. We had bad times together. Just like me, he's human. We all make mistakes, we do stuff, we don't think about consequences. We get lost and think that we're a god. I just hope . . . that he finds God and . . . that everything works out for him. I hope that doesn't stay on his conscience either."

After William was paroled from Donovan Correctional Facility in San Diego in 2009, he tried to run from his past at the same moment he tried to make up for lost time. "I was shooting speed every single day for about a year and a half and you could tell, but I couldn't notice. Everybody was like, 'Dude, you're a hundred and fifty pounds. Your eyes have black rings around them, you look like shit,' and I wouldn't believe them."

He admitted he needed to go to rehab after seeing his father cry in front of him for the first time. His parents desperately wanted to see him seek help. He calls it his Moment of Clarity. They took him to rehab that day.

William says his drug use might have been just a symptom. Looking back, he knows the drugs might have been his attempt to cope with his role and accountability in Nick's death. "The drugs suppressed the feelings."

But now that he's finally sober, one might wonder, who was going to win out? Capone, Scrappy, the Blanket, or Will? "Today,

I would say Will. It's not a name I was given [on the streets]. It was not a name that was *earned*. My birth name—it means something to me now. The other names? All they did was bring me problems in life. William, that's the name I'm going to die with."

William understands the skeptics, and he doesn't fault them. He says that he doesn't need anyone to believe a word he says. For William, his viewpoint is not about talking, it's about doing. "I don't need to say anything to my detractors who think I'm just trying to make myself look good. I live through my actions now. In NA, I'm mentoring guys getting out of prison. Learning to run my own business." He's not indignant when he answers. He's an open book and wants to expose the bad and the good.

"I've done my time. I have nothing to hide. I'm not hiding from anybody. I don't have an ego like I used to. Anything I say, I'm hoping it helps somebody. Because when I was younger, I really didn't listen to people. A lot of people tried to help me, and I didn't listen to them. I wish I could have gone back and listened to them. Because it would have saved a lot of hard times. They tell us [in NA], 'Give back to the person that's going through what you went through.' God will repay you in the end. I truly believe that."

He has one last point. "Condemn that twenty-year-old. That's not me anymore. I got what I deserved."

Jesse Rugge served a total of thirteen years, eleven in state prison. Today there are no detectives sitting across from him. No law enforcement trying to talk perspective to some shit-scared twenty-year-old trying to distance himself. No, today he's in an industrial studio in the arts district in downtown Los Angeles to give an on-camera interview. His interrogators are the amplifying lights of two LED panels that enhance every nuanced shift of Adam's apple and eyes tracking beneath closed lids that open only when he's ready to speak. "When you're younger, all you want to do is point. You want to not take responsibility in certain actions, you want to find fault in the relationship, or 'It's my parents.' . . . You don't know how to take responsibility. . . . And it was like really strange to sit there and go wait a second, I fucked up. I made the choice."

Jesse did two and half years in isolation. "There is a lot of deep soul-searching at that time and stuff like that, but still my maturity level was still not there enough. Still a little knucklehead . . . hardheaded. Very immature. I think where the transition started is . . . getting a life sentence."

Jesse rocks back in his chair. "I'll never forget T69730. I'll never fucking forget that number. . . . That's a number that will never leave me."

And yet, as much disdain as he feels for his years behind bars, he carries the same amount of gratefulness for them. "As much as I hated prison, I mean, I needed it, man. I fucking hate saying that and I'm sorry to use the *F* word, but it's just true.

"I was guilty of the murder." Because, to Jesse, he didn't do anything to stop it.

He recalls a story while he was incarcerated. "I remember telling this man . . . I just got denied [parole] again . . . I said, 'Man,

I was a coward.' He goes, 'You weren't a coward.' He says, 'Do you know the definition of a coward?' I said, 'What do you mean?' He said, 'A coward is a person that has all the tools to handle the situation at that time in your life and then chooses to do nothing about it. That's a coward.' He said, 'Dude, you're just ignorant. You weren't bred to do that. You weren't taught to go ahead and do something like that.' He said, 'In a situation like that of course someone is going to try and save their own life.' I was like sitting there, but something dawned on me—I *was* guilty. I was guilty of the situation."

When asked about the publicity his role in the case has garnered, Jesse neither celebrates nor revels in it. "There are no winners. Any time we do a crime there are no winners. It's the fact that, like, I never realized the lack of participation [in stopping it] killed that young man's life."

Today Jesse knows what piece of the puzzle he had been from the beginning, knows his inaction was just as terminal as if he had pulled the trigger himself.

He doesn't need the view from the driver's seat of that white van, nor does he seek the warm fuzz within a haze of bong smoke. Today he lifts clasped hands and raises his eyes: "For Nicholas. I own up for Nicholas."

He also talks about his last parole hearing. He was the only person "off his yard at Chino [California Institute for Men] going to board" that day at one o'clock in the afternoon.

"I remember sitting there, and they said, 'Are you going to speak today, Mr. Rugge?' And I said, 'Yeah, I'm going to speak.'

They said, 'Do you have anything to say now?' I said, 'Yeah . . . I'm guilty. I'm guilty of the murder.' That was the first time I ever said that, and it was super emotional."

Jesse looks down at his arms. He may not care if anyone believes a single word. "It gives me chills right now, because I never thought that I would say something like that. And I remember the victim's family. You know, Susan. I just remember her and everything of them saying this is the first time he's ever admitted it. And it was the first time, like, that they needed to hear it too. Regardless if I walk out of here, I said it and they needed to hear that." He acknowledges he was "a follower . . . a peon."

He cups his hands together, adamant. "I'm not going to live Nicholas's life in vain. I'm just done with that behavior."

Jesse has since traveled to Rikers Island to speak to the incarcerated about his life and poor decision-making. He has voiced his opinion that redemption doesn't start once you are released but the minute you are locked up. He has held poetry workshops with formerly incarcerated youth and desires to one day teach in juvenile hall with no cameras, no publicity, and certainly no Justin Timberlake, who played him in the movie *Alpha Dog*.

Jeff Markowitz has his own opinion on second chances. "Rugge never should have gotten out. He should have been convicted of murder. This is what we believe. He put tape over my son's mouth and face. And taped his hands behind his back." If Rugge was doing fine in prison but was permanently incarcerated, Jeff Markowitz would have no issue with that.

Jeff discloses what it was like at Rugge's parole hearing, remembering how Nick and Rugge once wrestled under the Christmas tree. "Even though Rugge was responsible for Nick's death, you have compassion for him. But you *fight that away* because we know the truth. Looking at him, it still didn't fix what he had done. He wasn't convicted of what he should have been convicted of."

Susan Markowitz adds, "I felt for his parents, but that doesn't undo 'dead.'" She believes second chances should be granted if you haven't taken a life.

Jeff states, "Unless you're in our shoes, it's difficult to understand."

When discussing the morning that Nick left home without telling anyone, Jeff reflects how the "last time we saw Nick he didn't trust us enough to show us what he had [Valium in his pocket]. That was very devastating." The one message he does voice: "You gotta know when to fight for your life and get the hell out. Look at certain gangster movies—they put you in a calming situation before they *take you out*. Nick's a perfect example of that." Susan adds that Nick was lulled into a "false sense of security. Even up until the last minute."

As far as second chances and their son, Ben Markowitz, Jeff states, "Ben has become a wonderful father and husband. There's always that possibility [for redemption]."

Susan reflects, "Ben has learned from his past." She believes it no longer personifies him. He's reset his trajectory in terms of attitude, beliefs, and values, thanks to being a father of four. "I'm feeling the love for Ben as I did my own son. And I've never voiced that before. And that is the truth."

Kirk Miyashiro also had thoughts on William Skidmore and Jesse Rugge, both of whom have been released. "I'll put it as this," he says with a deep pause. "God has given me multiple second chances. He's never given up on me. He's my savior. He's everything. If I have a God who's done that for me out of the billions of people in this world, why wouldn't I extend the same to someone else?

"That's where I come from. I am not perfect, no one is. *We* all have made mistakes, yet Christ has died on that cross for that reason. And it's undeniable to me.

"How I feel about those two men?" His tone softens but never wavers in conviction. "If they truly have repented, and have decided to change their lives to save others, then thumbs-up from me. Absolutely." *What an elder sees sitting, the young can't see standing.*

As far as Detective Valencia's feelings about second chances? "There's essentially a good and evil in this world. You didn't need to be taught that you didn't need to kill another human being. One of the struggles in the military is we're raised our entire lives thinking murder's wrong, the Bible says it's wrong, and then you join the military and they're like, 'Hey, we want you to go kill that guy.' And have no repercussions. It's the same growing up in any family or household. I don't care what your demographics are.

Killing is wrong. The way that poor child died is not cool. I am not selective—we're law enforcement—and can't be selective in the laws we choose to enforce."

In regard to William Skidmore and Jesse Rugge earning their release? "If the state says, 'Let 'em out,' let 'em out. I'm not upset about it and don't have to agree with it. They don't have to call Mark to find out if it's okay. I wish them the best, but it doesn't reverse what happened. It's murder. If it was your family or friend—it's hard to forgive.

"This is a life-altering event for *all* families involved."

Carey Evans also reflected on Nick's life, writing, "Over time, I think that I've developed a more nuanced view of the whole thing, and I can even in some ways empathize with how they ended up doing what they did to Nick. We've all been in situations where we've been too scared to make the right decision, either because doing the right thing is difficult, or we don't see a way out of making the wrong choice."

Carey adds, "I have been thinking a lot about my seventeen-year-old self, and it's amazing how little of myself today I see in him. I imagine that, were my seventeen-year-old self to meet me today, he would feel the same. I imagine this is probably not too far off from what most of the guys responsible for Nick's death feel. And it would even probably be quite similar to what Nick would feel if he were alive today. But yet we are all quite fundamentally shaped by what our selves of August 2000 did that led us to be where and who we are or (in Nick's case) aren't today."

Carey doesn't know if he believes in "second chances, per se. But I certainly believe in forgiveness."

Now a father himself, Carey believes Nick's greatest impact on him was how he's come away "with a greater sense of value of life from the whole thing."

He continues, "As for Nick, who is the real story here, memory has a funny way of shaping perception. The task of getting to the bottom of who he was isn't easy—because he was someone to each and every one of us, and our memories are shaped by the parts of himself that he let any of us see over the time we knew him. I suppose if you were to triangulate all the input you got from different people about him, he'd be somewhere in the middle of all of it."

It is drizzling at Lizard's Mouth. An overcast has set in that blurs the ocean into an indistinguishable gray.

Two hikers laugh en route and pass just on the other side of Nick's memorial, never taking notice. As darkness descends, a single lantern illuminates Nick's carved name. Instead of flowers, there are Susan's thoughts before it:

He's in my heart and soul every single moment. When I wake up or go to sleep. It will never ever ever—and I do mean ever—get better in regard to the gut-wrenching pain of just not having him here. And just thinking of whom his bride would be or what his babies would look like. Or what he would look like. It will never go away. And I think people

199

think the pain lessens—it does not. And I'm okay with that because every day that I think about him and have that pain it means that he was so worth loving and losing. What else could you possibly want to live for? It's a mother's gift to speak about her son.

Susan wishes to harness ache in a way that leaves enough room for something beautiful to bloom. Nick still lives in her and through her resolve. "Nothing will ever comfort me until I have my son in my arms." However, she urges, "You have to be compassionate and live life." And now it's her son tasking us. "This is what Nick would want."

ACKNOWLEDGMENTS

Nick Markowitz

With sincere thanks:

Susan Markowitz
Eve Porinchak
Fiona Simpson
Detective Mark Valencia
My family

Simon & Schuster
Valerie Shea
InsideOUT Writers/Prison Insight Program

SOURCES

Phone, Written, or In-Person Interviews

Eddy Bachman* (a pseudonym)

Carey Evans

Jesse James Hollywood

Ryan Hoyt

Jeffrey Markowitz

Susan Markowitz

Kirk Miyashiro

Jesse Rugge

William Skidmore

Detective Mark Valencia

Nick Markowitz's Diary

Read by Susan Markowitz

Superior Court of the State of California for the County of Santa Barbara Grand Jury Proceedings No. 1014465

Vols. I–III (Oct 23, 24, 25, 26, 30, 2000), grand jury transcripts.

Vols. I–IV (May 15, June 24, June 30, July 1, 2009) Jesse James Hollywood trial transcripts.

Books

Markowitz, Susan, with Jenna Glatzer. *My Stolen Son: The Nick Markowitz Story*. New York: Berkley Publishing Group, 2010.

Scott, Robert. *Most Wanted Killer*. New York: Pinnacle Books, 2010.

Websites

nicholasmarkowitz.com (memorial site)

Video interview in collaboration with Michel DeAscentiis and Stan Okumura at attn.com:

jamesblatt.com

Susan Markowitz Facebook page

Jesse Hollywood Facebook page

Newspaper Articles

Kelley, Daryl, Tina Dirmann, and Sue Fox. "Simi Man and 3 Others Appear in Court in Slaying of Teenager." *Los Angeles Times*, August 19, 2000.

Fox, Sue. "The Last Days of Nick Markowitz." *Los Angeles Times*, December 10, 2000.

Fox, Sue. "Kidnap Victim Could Have Fled, Witnesses Testify." *Los Angeles Times*, November 1, 2001.

Fox, Sue. "Murder Suspect Testifies His Confession Was a Lie." *Los Angeles Times*, November 9, 2001.

Guccione, Jean. "Killer Gets Death Penalty." *Los Angeles Times*, February 8, 2003.

Chu, Henry and Solomon Moore. "Fugitive Kept Low Profile in Quiet Brazilian Beach Town." *Los Angeles Times*, March 11, 2005.

Pacheco, Angel. "Witness Recounts Frightening Stay By Jesse James Hollywood." *Santa Barbara News Press*, May 27, 2009.

Meagher, Chris. "Jury Finds Hollywood Guilty of Murder and Kidnapping." *Santa Barbara Independent*, July 8, 2009.

Silverstein, Amy. "Jesse James Hollywood Sentenced to Life." *Santa Barbara Independent*, July 15, 2009.

Welsh, Nick. "Jesse Rugge, Markowitz Kidnapper, Released." *Santa Barbara Independent*, October 24, 2013.

ABOUT THE AUTHOR

Johnny Kovatch founded the InsideOUT Writers/Prison Insight Program in seven state prisons throughout California. He also teaches expressive writing to minors being tried as adults in juvenile hall. Originally from Ohio, he currently resides in Los Angeles.